Pygmy narrow-mouthed frog
(actual size)

Astonishing Animals

Extraordinary Creatures and the Fantastic Worlds They Inhabit

TIM FLANNERY & PETER SCHOUTEN

WITHDRAWN

Atlantic Monthly Press
New York

OTHER BOOKS BY THE AUTHORS
Possums of the World: A Monograph of the Phalangeroidea
Tree Kangaroos: A Curious Natural History with R. Martin & A. Szalay
A Gap in Nature: Discovering the World's Extinct Animals

TIM FLANNERY
Mammals of New Guinea
The Future Eaters: An Ecological History of the Australasian Lands and People
Mammals of the South West Pacific and Moluccan Islands
Watkin Tench, 1788 ed.
The Life and Adventures of John Nicol, Mariner ed.
Throwim Way Leg: Tree-Kangaroos, Possums, and Penis Gourds—On the Track of Unknown Mammals in Wildest New Guinea
The Explorers: Stories of Discovery and Adventure from the Australian Frontier ed.
The Birth of Sydney ed.
Terra Australis: Matthew Flinders' Great Adventures in the Circumnavigation of Australia ed.
The Eternal Frontier: An Ecological History of North America and Its Peoples
The Life and Adventures of William Buckley ed.
The Birth of Melbourne ed.
Joshua Slocum, Sailing Alone around the World ed.

PETER SCHOUTEN
Prehistoric Animals of Australia, S. Quirk & M. Archer eds.
The Antipodean Ark: Creatures from Prehistoric Australia, S. Hand & M. Archer eds.

First published in Australia in 2004 by The Text Publishing Company

Published simultaneously in Canada
Printed and bound in China through Bookbuilders, Hong Kong

FIRST AMERICAN EDITION

Library of Congress Cataloging-in-Publication Data

Flannery, Tim F. (Tim Fridtjof), 1956-
    Astonishing animals : extraordinary creatures and the fantastic worlds
they inhabit / Tim Flannery ; with illustrations by Peter Schouten.
        p. cm.
    ISBN 0-87113-875-1
    1. Vertebrates. 2. Vertebrates—Pictorial works. I. Title.

QL605 .F64 2004
590—dc22   2004051712

Book designed by Chong Wengho

Atlantic Monthly Press
841 Broadway
New York, NY 10003

04 05 06 07 08   10 9 8 7 6 5 4 3 2 1

To
Bert (Lambertus) Schouten
Father, Mentor, Artist

Contents

Life: A Brief Biography

by Tim Flannery

EVER SINCE the spark of life first flashed into existence on our planet, living things have expanded their domain, invading and making one habitat after another their own. The result has been a triumph of evolutionary change and a world of organisms so complex and varied that all living things should really be regarded as astonishing. Some living things, however, lead such different lives from the ones we have experience of that, from our narrow vantage point on the land, they appear almost alien. The ninety-seven creatures that populate these pages represent, in one way or another, the outer limits of life's progress, and astonishing creatures they are indeed.

Despite three and a half billion years of evolutionary invasion and advance, the realm of life remains circumscribed, for it's still only the skin of our heavenly sphere that is softened with a dusting of living things. The bacteria and other micro-organisms have ventured farthest. Some eke out an existence in the pores of rocks situated around ten kilometres in the Earth's crust, while others are regularly hoisted by winds and currents a similar distance into the upper atmosphere.

Multi-celled animals, however, can exist only in a small part of this life-zone, and vertebrates—the creatures that are the focus of this book—are even more limited in their distribution. Despite the fact that man has touched the Moon, and vultures have collided with passenger jets 11,300 metres above the Earth, vertebrates can thrive only in a zone that ranges from the bottom of the Marianas Trench (a depth of around 11.2 kilometres) to a height of around 6400 metres in the Himalayas. The record for deep-living is held by an unidentified flatfish which was glimpsed by two submariners through the tiny window of a submersible as it touched down at the deepest point on Earth. In contrast there is a small, dull bird known as the wall-creeper (*Typodroma muraria*) which hops about among the bare rocks and scree slopes that sherpa Norgay Tensing and Edmund Hillary traversed in order to conquer Mount Everest. It says much about our ignorance of this living planet that we cannot identify the fish glimpsed at the bottom of the ocean, and that the next deepest record of a fish is from two kilometres nearer the surface—an undistinguished bag-like creature known as *Bassogigas profundus*.

If these are the geographical extremes to which life has pushed, there are other extremes as well—extremes of diet, of reliance on mysterious senses, and of sexual attraction. And it is the vibrant success of living things and their myriad ecological niches that has inspired this book.

Before embarking on our investigation of these natural wonders it is necessary to trace life's long journey, from its obscure origins to its present success, for only then will we see these creatures in context. The expansion of life in time and space is, according to evolutionary biologist Michael Archer, 'the saga of a four-dimensional bio-blob' (the fourth dimension being time), which is forever ramifying, splitting and terminating at the ends as it weaves its way through the obstacle course of extinction and opportunity that Earth has provided. Because all life shares a single origin, that bio-blob had to begin somewhere, and at some specific time, yet our knowledge of these matters remains frustratingly dim. Even the fundamental issue of which planet life originated on cannot be resolved at present, for some astronomers hold firmly to the view that life began on Mars and was carried inside rocks blasted from the red planet's surface some four billion years ago.

Wherever its ultimate origin, life must have taken hold at a specific time and a specific place on the Earth's surface. It seems to have done this so long ago, however, that at our current remove in time we have little hope of pinpointing that origin. Almost no rocks survive from that distant period, and many of those that remain are so distorted by pressure and heat as to have destroyed all fossils. And, of course, any fossils would be microscopic and simple in structure. These difficulties, and many others, mean that we may be doomed to live with an uncertainty of hundreds of millions of years in pinpointing the moment that earthly life began.

Mapping the precise geographic origin of life looks equally hopeless. Perhaps its cradle was a contained environment—a saline pool or a sandy beach, for example—or perhaps it was an entire ocean. Even the type of environment likely to have nurtured life's first spark is contested by scientists. Some claim that the bottom of a frozen pool was the most likely spot, while others give the honour to volcanic vents in the ocean depths or the shores of the first oceans, where the sand acted as a sieve for the molecules that made life. The truth is we simply don't know.

Wherever and whenever it happened, we do know that by 3.5 billion years ago our earliest ancestors (along with the ancestors of all living things) had established themselves on planet Earth, because it's at this period that we find the earliest fossils. They are simple, single-celled

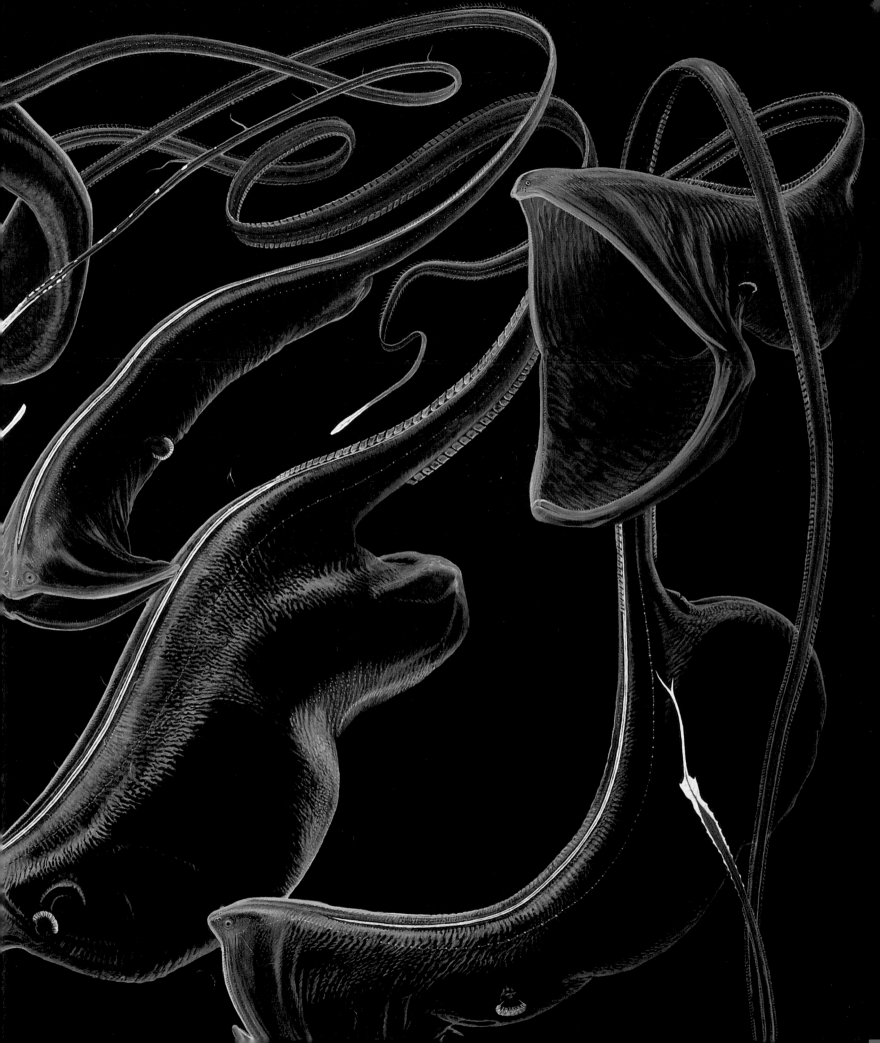

specimens, but they inform us unequivocally that life was in existence within a billion years of our planet's formation. Although considerable biochemical advances were made over the next three billion years, life remained microscopic. The first cells to possess a nucleus (where the chromosomes are stored) had evolved by 900 million years ago, and the sexual act was performed by them for the very first time. This last was a miraculous advance that greatly hastened life's progress, because sex gives life variety (by this I mean that children are not just clones of their parents), and out of variety evolution can forge new species.

By 700 million years ago life had spread through the shallow waters of the oceans forming a thin, living soup of varied, complex, yet still mostly microscopic things. Some organisms lay on the surface sediments and formed recognisable structures like algae-filled mounds and bacterial films. More complex hydra-like creatures perched among them, and the waters themselves were filled with tiny floating beings. Then, rather suddenly around 600 million years ago, the pace of change picked up again. The first complex animals—the so-called Ediacaran fauna—sprang into existence. Now, had you swum in those early shallow seas, you wouldn't have needed a microscope or magnifying lens to see life, for some Ediacaran creatures were true giants. One flatworm was nearly a metre long, while some seapens waved forty centimetres above the seafloor on which they were rooted.

The Ediacaran animals are diverse. As well as flatworms and seapens, some look like jellyfish while others resemble sea anemones. So obscure is their biology that researchers cannot agree on what they are, some claiming that even the most animal-like are nothing but bizarre marine lichens! Yet it is certain that they all lived suspended in the ocean's sunlit waters, or lay gently on the shallow sea floor. The Ediacaran animals thrived for 58 million years, but 542 million years ago a revolution occurred. Life evolved a wondrous new capacity—the ability to grow a hard coating, and with that came the ability to dig and burrow. Soon a great host of creatures were turning the ocean floor into a turmoil of burrows, troughs and pits. This was a major breakthrough, for now the ocean sediments themselves became a prime repository for life. From this point on, the ability of life to adapt and diversify accelerated markedly.

Around 420 million years ago plants began to grow on land, greening the moister parts of the continents, and by 400 million years ago came the first creatures to venture onto land— the scorpions and their relatives, which hitherto had dwelt in the sea. Within 20 million years of this signal event fishes began to gulp air and 15 million years later some of these gulpers

began to squirm out of the water and drag themselves through the shallows, eventually to colonise the dry land. Primitive insects crawled out of the sea at around the same time, and between 350 and 320 million years ago some began to develop wings, and so it was that life took to the air. From ocean to sediment to land and finally to air, life now occupied all of the major realms open to it, but still it continued to diversify, strengthening its grip, and giving our third planet from the Sun its unique signature.

A vital part of that process has been the creation of ever more living space for life, by life itself. Parasites have been perhaps the most direct beneficiaries, and they have become so prevalent and abundant that living bodies are almost like miniature planets colonised by ever tinier living things. By way of illustration, it's been estimated that 10 per cent of the human body—even a well-groomed one—is made up of cells belonging to non-human parasitic or symbiotic organisms. They are a host of aliens inhabiting our body that we cannot rid ourselves of or indeed live without, for many help us perform vital functions such as digestion.

So interwoven are the tendrils of life's four-dimensional bio-blob that Earth is considered by many scientists to be a single living entity that controls its temperature and the composition of its atmosphere so as to maintain optimum conditions for itself. The mechanisms are complex, but they include the photosynthesis of plants and the use of carbon by living things such as

coral reefs. Because carbon dioxide is a greenhouse gas, taking it out of the atmosphere affects the Earth's temperature. The scientist James Lovelock dubbed this great living, self-regulating entity Gaia, after the Greek personification of the Earth.

It is curious, though, that life has not leaped over all of the barriers that our planet has presented with equal alacrity. The various contexts in which life exists—water, the land's surface, the air, and in the sediments themselves—present very different challenges and opportunities. Let's consider that vital transition from water to land. The first step in making this transition was doubtless made by a fish, perhaps an inhabitant of a stagnant pond—and it involved gulping air. Thus the lung came before the leg by over 10 million years, but it was to take many more millions of years before other life functions could be performed by land animals. Judging from the habits of crocodiles (which must take their food into the water in order to swallow it), learning how to feed on land was a long and tortuous process. But it was reproducing in the absence of water that was the most difficult barrier to cross. The hard-shelled (amniote) egg was the key to success here, and it first appeared many tens of millions of years after the first fish hauled itself ashore.

The same sort of pattern can be seen in the transition from land to air. Although flying first evolved between 350 and 320 million years ago, to this day many flying creatures cannot feed while on the wing. And despite the 200 million years that have passed since the first vertebrate (a flying reptile known as a pterosaur) took to the air, not a single species has ever developed the talent of completing the reproductive cycle aloft.

We do not need to leave the solid surface of Earth to encounter many extreme and extraordinary environments, which even today remain virtually unexplored. Yet more people have been to the Moon than have been to the bottom of the ocean, and we know more about our satellite's dark side than we do of the creatures that inhabit the Marianas Trench. We think of the ocean—with its intense pressure, cold and eternal darkness—as an incredibly hostile place, though in reality it's the largest single habitat on Earth. Based on size, it is the land-dwellers that inhabit a marginal environment, and for the countless billions of creatures of the uncounted tens of thousands of species whose home is the ocean deep, conditions on land would seem as deadly and outlandish as those of outer space itself.

The changes life has made in order to survive in various environments are not always readily apparent to us. Consider the deep-sea fishes. Most people don't realise that many of them have pathetically weak skeletons and terribly flabby bodies—in extreme cases they're reduced to an almost gelatinous consistency, and seem to be composed merely of mouth and stomach. This is because so little food exists at such great depths that when it arrives it must be eaten come what may. Sometimes it arrives in the form of a creature larger than the predator itself, which accounts for the wicked-looking fangs and expandable stomachs of many deep-sea fish. This lack of food means that many deep-sea species do as little as possible between feeds in order to save energy. Researchers have discovered recently that parts of the deep ocean experience a 'rain' of debris from the sunlit layers above that coincides with the spring plankton bloom, which forms an annual bounty that must keep many species alive until the next 'rain'.

It is not necessary to live in the ocean depths for food to constrain your evolutionary development. The aye-aye (a lemur from Madagascar) and the great-tailed triok (a marsupial from New Guinea) eat similar foods—principally wood-boring grubs. Despite their very different origins they have evolved striking similarities of tooth, hand and tail in pursuit of their specialised diet. And a mammal (the long-beaked echidna), a bird (the kiwi) and a fish (a mormyrid) have come to share startling similarities through preferring a diet of worms.

Sex and magnificence are on intimate terms in the animal kingdom, sexual attractiveness being one of evolution's greatest imperatives. Most of the spectacular birds featured in this book are males. This is because when it comes to reproduction, in most species it is the female that makes the critical choice. The male must provide what the discerning female eye (or nose or ear) wants. As a result, male birds of paradise have transformed their bodies into glorious if sometimes bizarre sexual attractions, often at the expense of escaping predators and feeding efficiently. But what is most astonishing about them is not that they attract female birds of paradise, but that they affect human sensibilities as well—eloquent proof of the idea that the aesthetics of beauty are shared by an astonishing variety of living things; a result, perhaps, of our common genetic heritage.

Not all male sexual appurtenances, however, are attractive to humans. It's hard to discern the seductive powers of the 'standards' borne by the standard-wing nightjar. Perhaps the female chooses the males with the largest standard feathers because they represent the greatest handicap to their owner. Although this sounds nonsensical, it makes good evolutionary sense, for the bearers of such 'handicaps' are in effect proclaiming, 'Look at me! I've grown into a big strong male even while carrying these cumbersome handicaps, so my genes must be extra good. They will benefit your daughters, who will not bear my handicaps, while your son's handicaps will attract females as well!'

Despite our shared genetic heritage, our concept of beauty is largely dependent on the nature of our senses. We can appreciate the beauty of a bird of paradise because, like us, birds are visual creatures. For all their grotesquery, seadevils must be attractive to other seadevils, otherwise there would be none, though just where the attraction lies is beyond my reckoning. Perhaps it is scent, touch, or movement that makes the male seadevil swoon. Whatever it is, it's a near-fatal attraction, for the male seadevil is tiny compared with his mate, and when he encounters her he does not seek to copulate, but instead bites her, never to let go. The two grow together, and in some species the male's head becomes embedded in the body of the female. Nurtured solely by her blood, he becomes nothing but a dependent testicle that is somehow instructed by the female (perhaps through hormones) to release sperm at her command.

While the need for sex can lead to truly astonishing adaptations, a need for security can also manifest itself in the most intriguing evolutionary strategies. The humble shield-tailed agama lizard has transformed its tail into a knobby door-stopper, while the flamboyant crest of the sail-tailed lizard may help it leap to safety. Vanishing is another form of defence. The bay owls are so good at it that one species, the African bay owl, remained unknown to science until 1951 when a single specimen was found. It was 1996 before another one was sighted. Some fish have elevated vanishing to an art form. The most spectacular disappearing acts are performed by pipefish and seadragons, yet outside their environment they are among the most flamboyant creatures imaginable. Some animals have even been driven to ignominy by their need to hide—witness the screaming Budgett's frog, which looks like a turd left by a tapir at a waterhole.

We hope that this book provides an opportunity to consider animals outside the everyday perception of their place, and that of other creatures, in nature. Firstly consider how a dog lives—through its nose: tracking people by scent along a busy street, 'smelling' illnesses such as cancer and somehow anticipating earthquakes, yet all the while seeing the world myopically in black and white. To imagine the very different life of the hairy seadevil, however, does lift us into another realm, for not only is its sex life bizarre but its habitat is too. Imagine living at pressures that would crush us in an instant, in a world of impenetrable darkness and frigid cold, where there exists no edges or ends—just an eternity of space.

When imagining such realms, remain alert, for things are not always what they seem. Even this book has its own trap. One of the creatures depicted here does not exist at all outside the imagination. I wonder if you can discover which one it is?

The Vertical Terrain

THERE ARE a few places on Earth where you can stand on a mountain summit five kilometres above the sea and look down across a panorama of snow, alpine meadow, alpine rainforest, mountain rainforest, lowland jungle and beach. It is a similar situation to standing on the North Pole and seeing the equator. These multiple habitats stacked on the mountainside offer different opportunities for life. In open places, ultraviolet light, which is invisible to us, is utilised by birds to make their courtship displays more brilliant. In other places, at certain times, sound carries exceptionally well, providing other opportunities to courting species which use acoustics to advertise for a mate.

Where temperatures are warm, soils fertile and sunlight abundant, food abounds, allowing for the most extravagant and energy-expensive displays to flourish. In places where it is cold, cloudy or infertile, a shortage of resources forces species to develop unusual reproductive strategies. Here are examples along a transect from the world's highest mountains to the sea, which offer a glimpse of some of the more unusual creatures and how they live.

Himalayan monal

(Lophophorus impejanus)

AS SUMMER warms the high Himalayas in Nepal, melting the snow in the upper meadows, an unusual kind of pheasant known as the Himalayan monal undertakes a great vertical migration. From their winter refuges in forests at around 2000 metres these turkey-sized birds scramble and fly to alpine grasslands above the tree-line where, at up to four and a half kilometres above sea level, they feed and nest. It's easy to tell when monals are about, for their feeding pits pockmark the meadows. These pits, which are made in their search for insects, tubers and roots, are excavated by the bird's powerful beak, and are often up to twenty-five centimetres deep.

The bird here is a male in full display. There are thirty-five species of pheasants, some of which are well-known game birds. Other, lesser-known species, however, are among the most spectacular of all birds. The peculiar wiry crest of the Himalayan monal resembles an exotic headdress. Displaying males are at their best in April and May, and when viewed in the full sunlight of their open habitat, the metallic iridescence of their plumage must be truly breathtaking. Remember too that when seen through the ultraviolet-sensitive eyes possessed by all birds, the male Himalayan monal must be one of the most vivid sights in nature.

Ribbon-tailed astrapia
(Astrapia mayeri)

MOUNTAINS AND spectacular birds seem to go together, and no place on Earth is as amply blessed with both as the island of New Guinea. The ribbon-tailed astrapia inhabits a tiny region of Papua New Guinea's highlands in the vicinity of Mount Hagen. This bird of paradise has the longest tail feathers relative to body size (over three times longer) of any bird, but despite its dramatic appearance it was the last bird of paradise to be discovered by Europeans. The first scientific description was based on two tail feathers plucked from a native headdress in the 1930s, the bird itself remaining hidden in its mountain fastness until 1939, when at last a whole skin arrived at the Australian Museum in Sydney.

Ribbon-tailed astrapias hop about in the mossy forest canopy in search of insects and the fruit of mountain trees and shrubs, and as with many birds of paradise they have bright feathers around the beak. As might be imagined, the male's extraordinary tail feathers are sometimes difficult to control, and occasionally flap wildly about in the breeze as the bird tries to feed. They do take great care of the streamers, however, for they are vital to courtship. As part of the mating ritual males have been observed spreading a wing and flicking their tails, before flying

upwards to a perch in the sunlit canopy, the tails becoming a glittering streamer that makes them look like a comet. For all we know this might be the entire display—perhaps the females are not so choosy about their courtship. After all, it must be easy to pick the male with the longest tail, and with tail feathers like that what else could a female ribbon-tailed astrapia want?

Satyr tragopan

(Tragopan satyra)

THE TRAGOPANS are members of the pheasant family, five species of which inhabit the Himalayas and central China. The satyr tragopan is a mountain dweller, living in the oak and rhododendron forests of the Himalayas where there is dense undergrowth. There it searches for the insects, leaves, sprouts and seeds that are its principal food.

The inflatable bib (called the lappet) and the 'horns' of the males are erectile organs, which are distended by an increased flow of blood when the bird becomes excited. Named for its 'horns', the satyr tragopan exhibits the greatest engorgement of all tragopans. And it's a bit of a show-off, lying in wait behind a log or rock, and popping up like a jack-in-the-box when the female draws near.

It is often the case among birds that a gorgeous cock is a poor provider. Beautifully adorned males may put on a wonderful courtship, but all too often contribute nothing to the raising of the chicks, leaving that duty to the dull hen-birds. The satyr tragopan is a stand-out exception here, for not only is he dashingly handsome but he seems to be monogamous and a dutiful father as well. The female lays two to six eggs, which are incubated for twenty-five to twenty-eight days, and thereafter the father contributes equally to the upbringing and care of the young.

Resplendent quetzal
(Pharomachrus mocinno)

THE RESPLENDENT quetzal is arguably the most beautiful bird in all of the Americas. Its face is almost chick-like, giving it that cute appeal which draws such a strong response from humans. An inhabitant of the mossy mountain forests of southernmost Mexico, its glittering, metallic feathers change colour with the light, appearing to the human observer to be either green or blue as the clouds pass overhead. Although strikingly similar in appearance to some of New Guinea's birds of paradise there are marked differences, for the female resplendent quetzal is as beautiful as her mate (though only he has the long tail) and both the male and female incubate the eggs. This duty, however, can give the male some trouble, for he must turn carefully when entering the cramped nest to avoid damaging his splendid train. Its call is a steady *k'yow-k'yow.*

The creature is the sacred bird of the Mayans, and was considered to be the spiritual protector of Mayan chiefs. Legend has it that when the Spanish attacked the Mayans in 1524 the quetzal appeared and pecked

at the leader of the invading army. At the moment the Mayan chief died, the quetzal fell silent and plummeted to Earth, covering the chief's body. That night the bird's colours were transformed—its chest is now the colour of royal Mayan blood. Today it is the national bird of Guatemala, also lending its name to that country's currency.

The quetzal is as delicate as it is beautiful, and it is known in museums around the world as a taxidermist's nightmare. So fragile are its feathers and so impermanent their red pigmentation that museum specimens are often a pale imitation of the living bird.

Marvellous spatuletail

(Loddigesia mirabilis)

HUMMINGBIRDS ARE tiny, jewel-like creatures that often have wonderful common names such as sunangels, emeralds and spatuletails—names inspired by the wonderfully iridescent feathers characteristic of these creatures. The marvellous spatuletail, however, has an additional claim to fame, for it is the only bird in the world that has just four feathers in its tail. But what feathers they are! In the adult male two of them form splendid blue rackets nearly three times the length of their owner's body, which cross each other and end in purplish blue discs. The male pulls one racket at a time above its head, where the highly iridescent discs at their ends—doubtless a fine reflector of ultraviolet light—form an irresistible lure to the female.

These tail feathers are permanent and not, as with the display feathers of many species, shed at the end of the breeding season. This means their owners must expend a large amount of energy dragging them about. The creature inhabits a 100-kilometre stretch of forest on the right bank of the Rio Utcubamba in Peru, a region that abounds with nectar-producing flowers in order to support such an extravagant, nectar-feeding creature.

King of Saxony bird of paradise

(Pteridophora alberti)

WHEN THE first specimens of this creature were dispatched to the museums of Europe in the late nineteenth century, one of the world's most eminent ornithologists, Professor Bowdler-Sharpe, airily dismissed them as an obvious fake—the creation of some crafty taxidermist. Had he seen a living bird he would have been astonished, for the brow plumes that gave the

professor pause, which are over twice the length of the bird's body, are put to vigorous use in nature.

The king of Saxony bird lives high in New Guinea's mossy mountains where, in certain places, the morning and evening air is filled with a buzzing, fizzling sound resembling that made by a malfunctioning electric motor. This is the call of the male king of Saxony bird. I once saw a male display within a couple of metres of me. It flew onto a vine crossing a jungle path, upon which it jumped up and down until the vine was in motion like a swing. As it called, it slowly erected its brow feathers, first making them stand at 90 degrees to the body before bringing them fully forward. In this pose it resembled a gigantic longicorn beetle.

Males display head-on to females, which means that she would perceive her mate as being at the end of a corridor of enamel-blue 'flags' formed by his brow feathers—the 'enamel' surface of the blue flags is on the inside of the feathers when they are brought forward. These flags fluoresce in ultraviolet light, thereby adding to their brilliance in the female's eyes.

Black sicklebill

Black sicklebill

(Epimachus fastuosus)

WHY DOES one species of bird rely on sound to attract a mate, while another uses brilliant colours? We have no answer to the question at present, though we do know that birds of paradise excel at both, with the black sicklebill bird of paradise producing one of the most distinctive acoustic-based courtship displays in nature.

As dawn begins to lighten the eastern horizon in New Guinea's mountains, the male black sicklebill perches on a branch overhanging a ravine or valley and prepares to turn himself into a machine for amplifying sound. Because the air is still, sound carries much further now than later in the day, when currents disrupt the sound waves. The transformation from bird to amplifier is achieved with the assistance of an extraordinary suite of feathers that look like a set of false wings, and which when raised form a collar-like parabolic reflector.

Marshalling all its vocal powers, the bird utters a series of explosive calls. *Buk! Buk!* The sound carries out over the valley, and any listening female must perceive the calls as emanating from a strange, metre-long object, black but highly reflective—more of a space-age design than a living bird. It is only when she approaches, drawn by his call, that she would see his glorious violet and aqua colours.

Blue bird of paradise

(Paradisaea rudolphi)

THE BLUE bird of paradise has been acclaimed by ornithologists as the most beautiful bird in the world. Certainly the display of this crow-sized creature is one of the most outrageous performances ever devised by nature. The male prefers to display in the afternoon—between 12.30 and 5.30 pm—and unique among the birds of paradise he dances upside down, hanging from a branch. As he begins his display, he flexes, sending waves of blue and violet shimmering through his feathers. At the centre of his chest is a dark oval patch lined on its lower margin with red. This is rhythmically expanded and contracted so that it resembles a huge, slowly expanding eye whose effect, even on humans, is hypnotic. All the while the performer's own eyes are closed, revealing white eyelids, which lend him an unearthly air.

As he reaches the climax of his display, he utters a call described by an experienced ornithologist as 'incredible'—an intense, rhythmic buzzing with an electric quality, the pulsing of which he synchronises with the pulsing of his body. It is this that the female finds irresistible, and if one is nearby she will now approach the male and allow copulation to take place.

The frenetic display of the male blue bird of paradise clearly indicates that he has energy to burn in the pursuit of love, and indeed it lives in the richest zone of the forest, between 1000 and 2000 metres, where food is abundant and reliable.

Blue bird of paradise

Superb bird of paradise

(Lophorina superba minor)

WHY THE island of New Guinea should be home to so many amazing looking birds is an interesting question, for not only is it home to nearly all birds of paradise, but the world's largest pigeon and many kinds of bowerbirds. With the exception of a few small marsupials the island has no native carnivorous mammals, which is perhaps why New Guinea's birds get away with more extravagant displays than birds elsewhere.

The superb bird of paradise is probably the most common of all, for it is found at middle elevations from one end of New Guinea to the other, where it feeds on fruits, berries, seeds and insects. It can survive in disturbed habitats, and is relatively unwary and conspicuous, so it is likely to be seen even by casual visitors. But one would have to be fortunate indeed to see a male in the full frenzy of his display. He performs on a log or rise in an opening in the forest, and early in his performance might dangle from a twig by the neck with his cape thrust forwards, looking as if he has hanged himself.

At the height of his courtship he utterly transforms his upper body to become a reflective bowl that encircles his head with the brilliant feathers of the breast-shield and the cape of long feathers on his neck. If seen from head-on, two brilliant green false eyes appear to stare from the bottom of the bowl. In this posture the male dances a short-stepping, jerky fandango—rather like the movements of a fencer—around the enchanted female, his parabola reflecting both light and sound towards the object of his desire.

Bulwer's pheasant

(Lophura bulweri)

WHEREVER THEY have escaped the chainsaw, the primeval forests of Borneo cast such a dense shadow that below the canopy lies a realm of eternal, gloomy twilight. So, if you live there, what better way to attract a mate than with a brilliant white disc, shimmering like a sun in the leaf-littered underworld? Bulwer's pheasant, a very large and handsome bird found only on Borneo, uses just this strategy. But the pheasants are distributed widely in the forest, so it is tricky to ensure that a female is close enough to see the disc. To initially attract a prospective mate, throughout the mating season the male utters a sharp, penetrating cry—like a shrill scream. At other times, perhaps for fear of attracting clouded leopards or other predators, he satisfies himself with a metallic *kook kook*, or nervous *kak kak*.

As the female approaches she sees the most extraordinary sight, a side-on view of his great white disc of a tail, glowing like the full moon in the dark of the forest. When he sees her, the male falls silent, so that the scratching sound of the small spines on the bottom of his tail can be heard as they scrape on dead leaves. Perhaps this slight noise reminds her of the clatter of little bird-feet in the forest litter, or the sound of chicks feeding. Whatever the case, she finds the entire display irresistible and soon little Bulwer's pheasants are incubating in their eggs. Just why the male possesses such a sinister looking mask, however, remains a mystery.

Long-wattled umbrella bird

(Cephalopterus penduliger)

THE LONG-WATTLED umbrella bird is a bizarre member the Cotingidae family of birds which is only found in South and Central America. This bird's habitat is very restricted, as it is found only on the seaward slopes of some mountains in western Colombia and Ecuador, and even there it is only found where forests are undisturbed. Because it is large and spectacular in appearance, the long-wattled umbrella bird is an easy target. It migrates up and down the mountains during certain periods of the year, making it more liable to encounter hunters who can quickly exterminate it. Only a few populations live within protected areas, making it one of the rarest and most endangered birds on earth.

Long-wattled umbrella birds are poor fliers, and as they patter about in the canopy with their crests laid flat, pursuing on foot the insects and fruit that make up their diet, the females resemble crows. The males are twice as large as females and this, combined with the male's wattle, makes the sexes look almost like different species. This wattle is thirty-five centimetres long and is covered in short, square-ended, scale-like feathers. It is without doubt rather cumbersome and must serve some function, but strangely no one has recorded seeing it put to use. During the breeding season the males utter a loud, booming call, but details of mating and courtship remain unknown. Its nest was first seen by scientists in 2003, and as yet details of it have not been published.

Wilson's bird of paradise

(Cincinnurus respublica)

MALES OF the genus *Cincinnurus* are as close as any creature comes to being a living jewel. They are the smallest members of the bird of paradise family, and some have very limited distributions. Wilson's bird, for example, is found only on the islands of Salawatti and Batanta, which lie off the north-western end of New Guinea. There, in a sunlit clearing kept clean and tidy, in close proximity to a fallen tree, the male dances with a carefully selected leaf in his beak, all the while puffing out his handsome green breast shield in a rhythmic pulsing motion.

Much of the male's jewel-like ornamentation reflects ultraviolet light, which perhaps explains why he chooses a sunlit 'court' in which to display. When the sun hits the perch the ultraviolet reflects off his yellow cape, his breast shield and long, curly violet tail feathers, which he cocks to the same angle as his cape to maximise reflectivity.

To see what the spectrum of visible light reveals of his display, travel by dugout canoe to the south coast of Batanta Island. Once there, disembark on a white beach of coral sand and walk into the cool of the forest. An important discovery is waiting to be made there, for the nest and eggs of this marvellous bird have never been reported.

Wilson's bird of paradise

Standard-wing nightjar
(*Macrodipteryx longipennis*)

OBSERVERS SAY that during the breeding season, when a male standard-wing nightjar takes to the air, he resembles a hawk being mobbed by a pair of drongos. The 'drongos' are his great standard-feathers, which move in a most peculiar fashion as he flaps his wings. Their strange action—they assume a vertical position and swing about—must be the result of air currents, for there are no muscles to lift them and they lie flat when the bird is on the ground.

No male is acceptable to a female without these great standards, though why the females should find them desirable is mysterious. They clearly serve a role in courtship, however, for they are an inconvenience in every other respect. Once the breeding season finishes, the males promptly nip them off. Whatever their evolu-

tionary origins and attraction to the opposite sex the birds are doing something right, for standard-wing nightjars remains common over a large swathe of central and northern Africa.

To see this amazing bird in full breeding regalia you will probably need to forgo the Christmas feast of roast turkey and plum pudding and instead travel to Africa's Gold Coast or Congo. A glimpse of them might be possible later in the year in Sudan or Ethiopia, when they migrate north, but by then they are, alas, *sans* standards.

Wallace's standard-wing

(Semioptera wallacei)

NEARLY ALL birds of paradise are restricted to New Guinea or its nearby islands, but Wallace's standard-wing inhabits the famed Spice Islands of eastern Indonesia. The largest of these islands is known as Halmahera and, along with nearby Batchan, it forms the birds' only home. In the days of Sir Francis Drake Halmahera was known as Jailolo, and was a famed 'spicerie'. Today a town on Halmahera's west coast still bears the name Jailolo, and a few kilometres inland from this historic settlement, in a patch of deep jungle, is a rough wooden hut with a sign above it proclaiming it to be the 'bird friendship house'. Here it is possible to see the *Semioptera*, or signal-wing as its name translates from Latin.

The males of this crow-sized bird gather in a particular forest tree, presumably chosen for its height, location and open canopy; and there, just before dawn, they begin to display. As the first morning light appears in the east they call raucously, then leap vertically a metre or so from their perch with their brilliant green breast shield erect, all the while raising and lowering their prominent white standard feathers. When a dozen or more males display they resemble a crowd of jumping, cheering football fans. In the dawn darkness, the white 'standards' are the most striking part of this display, and somehow, out of the gaggle of males, the female makes her choice.

As with all birds of paradise, all the male contributes to his offspring is a brief mating, the burden of building the nest, incubating the eggs and bringing up the chicks falling to the female. Only in the richest of environments, such as that offered by the East Indian spiceries, could a solitary parent succeed in doing this, and only in such an environment could a male devote such time and energy to the pursuit of sex.

Calfbird

(Perissocephalus tricolor)

THE MALES of many species get together to do things that attract females—just think of rock bands and football clubs—but when male calfbirds join forces they put on a display that is unique in the animal world. These large relatives of the umbrella birds inhabit lowland tropical forests of northern South America, and there the males choose a tree for their activities. Once satisfied about the tree's suitability they strip it of leaves, creating a bare, skeletal stage on which their antics will be seen easily. Then each individual chooses a perch which they will rarely leave until the breeding season is finished.

Once a dozen or so male calfbirds have assembled, they stand around in dignified silence. After some time first one, then another, will lean forward, take a deep inward breath and emit a *grr* sound. Then, one by one they raise themselves erect on their legs and emit a solemn *moo* or *grauwww*, at the same time puffing up the feathers around their shoulders and head to form a cowl. With the last of the 'oo' part of the call, they lose their erect posture, slumping and then slowly leaning backwards until the last croak is emitted from a deflated creature leaning back on its perch at an angle of 15 degrees from the vertical.

Why do female calfbirds find this cartoon-comic display attractive? The brilliant colours favoured by ultraviolet-reflecting species such as the birds of paradise are less common in the lowland forests than mountain regions, perhaps because there is less light in the lowland forests. Maybe, amid all the life, sound and activity there, it takes a truly bizarre, communal display to be noticed.

Motion Specialists

GETTING about is the hallmark of most animal life. It is one of the most important things that animals do, for it allows them to find food, shelter and mates, and some species have developed astonishing powers of locomotion. There are squirrels that 'fly', marsupials that hop, and fish that walk. Such achievements allow these breakthrough species to proliferate, invade ecological niches unavailable to their competitors and, on occasion, give rise to entire new dynasties of organisms. Here is a small cast of innovators—species that get about in unexpected ways. They have been chosen to illustrate some of the unique challenges they face, and also the unexpected turns that their evolution has sometimes taken.

Woolly flying squirrel
(Eupetaurus cinereus)

GLIDING MAMMALS possess a broad membrane of skin that stretches between their legs, and is attached along the sides of their bodies. This parachute allows them to travel considerable distances through the air and probably first developed among tree-dwelling animals that leapt from branch to branch. It has proved to be a highly successful survival strategy, for many unrelated mammals have adopted it and flourished. While clearly suited to a life in the forest, some gliders have forgone their ancestral habitat and moved to life in the most unlikely of places. One such glider is the woolly flying squirrel of northern Pakistan—which has a chosen terrain of high cold desert, steep cliffs,

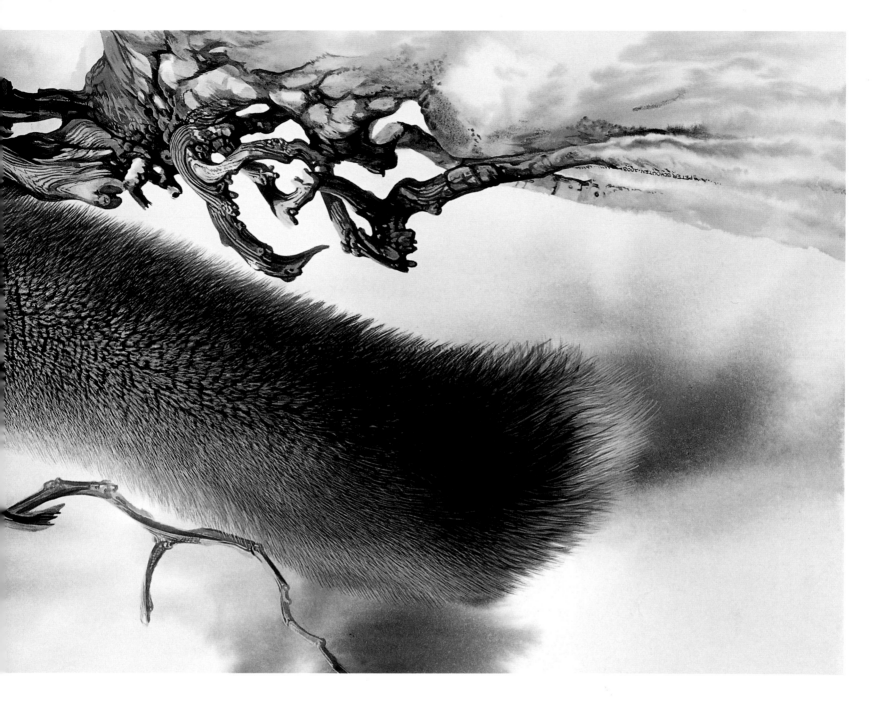

caves and rock slopes. The metre-long squirrels survive in this hostile region by feeding upon pine needles from scrubby alpine conifers that grow on the snow-strewn slopes. They presumably exercise their gliding membranes (which can be folded against the body and hidden when not in use) by volplaning from clifftops and boulders to escape danger or search for food. As its name suggests the woolly squirrel has an exceptionally dense fur—a vital asset in its frigid habitat. The animal is held in high regard by the mountain tribes as it provides them with a medicinal material known as salagit. They do not hunt the squirrel, but instead collect the salagit, which is thought to derive from its urine, from mountain caves. Its main threat is deforestation of the high slopes.

Colugo

(*Cynocephalus variegatus*)

HAVE YOU ever wondered how the first bats began to fly? The colugo provides some ideas, for it spends most of its life upside down, hanging from a branch as it feeds, walks and sleeps. It is also the most accomplished of all volplaners.

Inhabitants of the rainforests of south-east Asia, colugos eat leaves, buds and fruit. They are relics of an earlier age, for 50 million years ago their relatives could be found as far afield as Canada. With a volplaning membrane that stretches from its neck to the tip of its tail and on to its feet, the colugo has taken gliding to an extreme; so efficient is it that in a glide to a tree 130 metres away it loses just ten metres of elevation—not bad for a creature weighing more than one and a half kilograms.

Its extreme adaptation has led to compromises, however, for in order to defecate without

soiling its fur the colugo must hang from its hands and invert its tail. This is an awkward and seemingly perilous posture, and as with humans it probably takes some time for young colugos to be toilet-trained. The colugo has a single pair of teats in its armpits, and the young are nurtured within their blanket-like gliding membrane. Its fur is very fine, and is cleaned with the use of specialised incisors which are like combs, each one with up to twenty fine 'prongs' arising from the one root.

Namdapha flying squirrel

(Biswamoyopterus biswasi)

PAKISTAN AND northern India are home to a remarkable diversity of giant flying squirrels—indeed the region is world headquarters for these little-known creatures. And in 1981 the scientific world was astonished at the discovery of yet another species from this area. At a metre long from nose to tail tip, the beautiful Morocco-red creature was located in a small forest relic near Namdapha in the Tirap district of India's Arunchal Pradesh state. There have been no further sightings since the capture of the original male specimen, and scientists believe that no more than 250 individuals survive in this rapidly degrading habitat. In the case of the Namdapha flying squirrel, if you lose the trees you will lose the squirrel, an outcome which, given the rate of deforestation in India, cannot be long coming. And

42

when the Namdapha flying squirrel vanishes, gone too will be its secrets of survival—what it ate, how it reproduced, and how it lived in its forest home—a million years of hard-won evolutionary knowledge erased in an instant.

Black dorcopsis

Black dorcopsis

(Dorcopsis atrata)

GOODENOUGH ISLAND is a three-kilometre-high mitre of rock that projects out of the sea off New Guinea's east coast. Until a team of biologists climbed to its mist-shrouded, rainforested summit in the 1950s, nobody apart from the islanders suspected that it might be the only home of a very strange member of the kangaroo family. The black dorcopsis is a living fossil, a primitive relic of a bygone age when rainforest covered much of Australia. Many individuals have white 'sox' on one or both of their front paws, and a white tail tip, which contrast strongly with the black body fur.

The black dorcopsis spends its days hopping through the dense vegetation, seeking leaves, fruit and possibly the occasional insect. Perhaps for fear of leeches, it never lays the full length of its tail on the ground, instead letting only the tip contact terra firma. Not only is this animal one of the last members of the kangaroo family to be discovered, it is also one of the rarest and least studied. Its entire habitat covers less than 100 square kilometres, and it is avidly hunted by the islanders, which means that it is probably one of the most endangered as well.

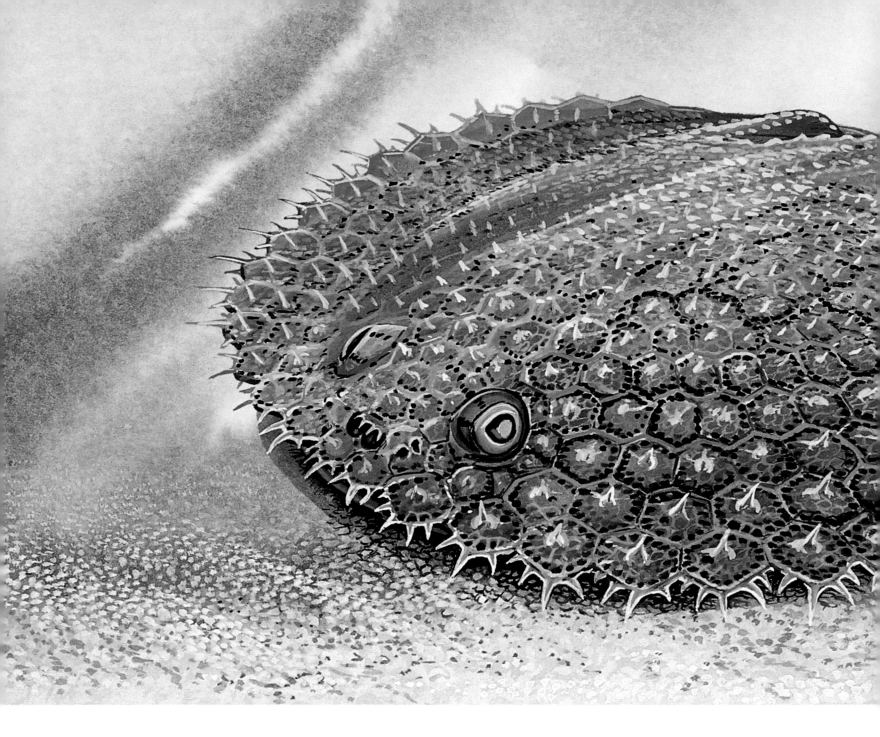

Starry batfish

(Ogcocephalus stellata)

THE FIRST starry batfish to come to the attention of scientists was a wee creature—just five centimetres long—which was dredged up in 1902 from a depth of over 400 metres near the Hawaiian Islands. It doubtless caused the scientists some excitement, for this fish can walk with its four limb-like fins, and can also jet propel itself from gill-slits on its sides. Adults, which can reach thirty centimetres in length, are as hard as a rock, their skin being reinforced with interlocking bone plates so as to resemble a flattened sea urchin. Although they can also swim in the conventional manner, starry batfish prefer to stroll about on the sea floor. They live at depths exceeding 300 metres throughout the tropical and subtropical regions of the Indian and Pacific oceans. Aside from these details, little more is known about them.

Mysore slender loris

(Loris tardigradus lydekkerianus)

THIS LEMUR-LIKE primate inhabits thorny acacia forest in the Bangalore region of southern India, where it creeps about among the thorns by night. It moves in a slow, deliberate manner, always keeping its grasp on the branchlets with at least three of its limbs. Curiously, it sticks to the upper side of branches (never hanging on from below), and while it can run on the ground it cannot swim.

Although they eat a lot of fruit, slender lorises are the ultimate stealth predators, moving almost imperceptibly towards lizards and other small creatures before making a lightning grab with both hands. They are extremely antisocial, and if kept together signal their discontent with growls, squeals and whistles.

Sulawesi naked bat

(Cheiromeles parvidens)

THE SULAWESI naked bat inhabits the lowlands of Sulawesi and some Moluccan islands. As it emerges from its roost just before dusk to hawk over forests and beaches, this spectacular bat looks like a gigantic swift. It is only on close examination, however, that it becomes clear just what a strange creature it is. The only hair noticeable on its body is found on the outer edge of the big toe, and inside a pouch on the throat. The hairs on the toe are stiff, strongly curved bristles, and seem to act as a comb to remove parasites. This is very useful, for Sulawesi naked bats are often crawling with a large species of earwig which lives nowhere else, and which must be very annoying—rather like having a parasite the size of a kitten crawling on your body.

The wings are exceptionally long and narrow—almost like the wings of a jet-fighter—and are adapted for rapid, direct flight. And as with some jets they can be conveniently folded away into pouches on the sides of the body. With its wings protected the bat is able to scurry about on the forest floor, where it finds much of its food.

With its massive teeth and hideous appearance this large bat—which has a body around the size of a starling—is some people's worst nightmare. Yet it is a gentle creature that never attempts to bite, even when very scared.

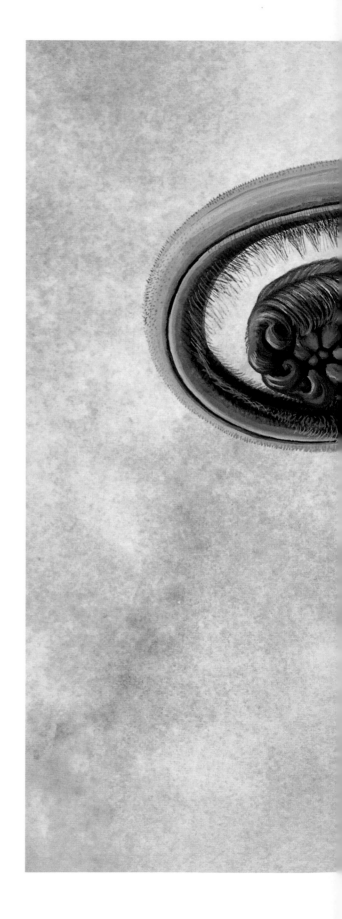

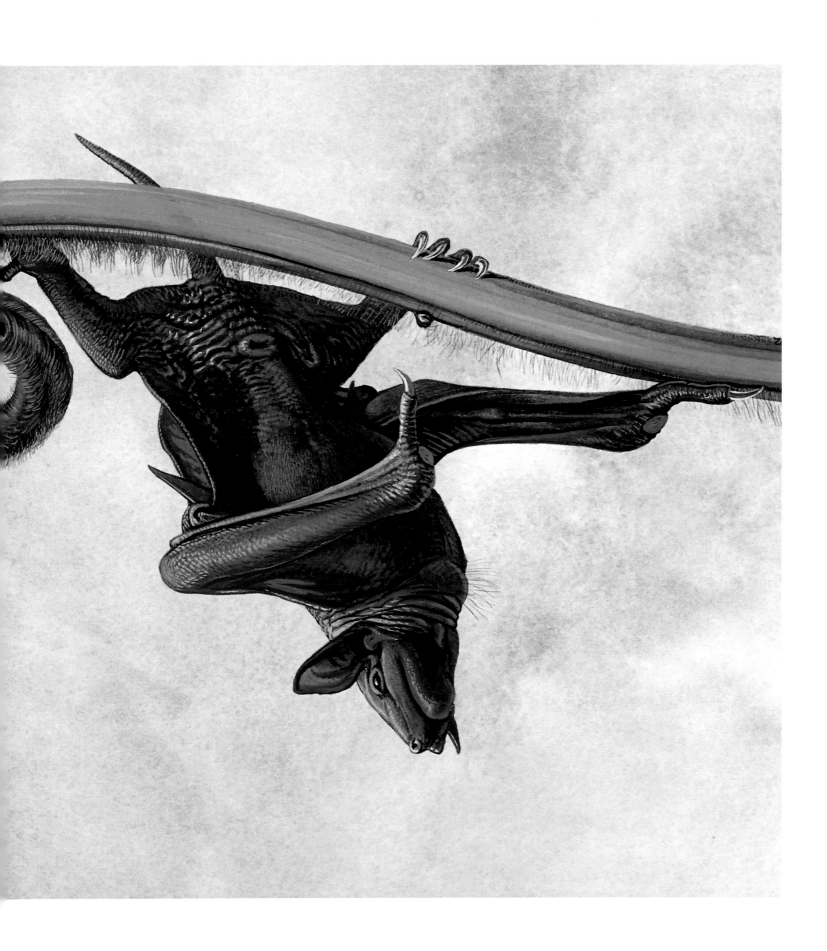

Food & Feeding

THEY SAY that you are what you eat, though in evolutionary terms it is more correct to say that what you eat will inevitably shape you. Species that consume difficult-to-digest, low-nutrient foods such as leaves can become sluggish and pot-bellied, for they live on tight energy budgets and need capacious stomachs in which to ferment their food. Worm eaters, on the other hand, are likely to develop a beak-like face so that they can probe in the earth for their slippery fare. Termite eaters, too, often develop long faces, and are liable to lose their teeth into the bargain.

Some unfortunate creatures pick through faeces for their food, and they have often become bald. That's because faeces is sticky and unhealthy, and feathered heads are far harder to keep clean than bald ones. Even stranger, at first glance, is the propensity for grub eaters to develop skeletal fingers; but these prove very useful for removing wood-boring grubs from their burrows.

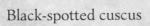
Black-spotted cuscus

Black-spotted cuscus

(Spilocuscus rufoniger)

THE BLACK-SPOTTED cuscus is the most brilliantly coloured of all marsupials. Only the males have a mottled pattern of black and white on their backs; the females (as shown) are of a vivid solid colour and have a large black saddle instead. Each male has a unique pattern of mottling, making individuals instantly recognisable at a distance, much like a human face does for us. Male cuscuses are often found perched atop the highest forest trees of New Guinea. Native hunters climb up to the possum's high perch and scan the canopy to locate other males—competitors perhaps—that the captured possum was doubtless keeping an eye on.

At almost seven kilograms, the black-spotted cuscus is around the size of a koala. It is the very largest of New Guinea's cuscuses, and found only in the northern lowland rainforests, where it prefers the old growth forest and its fruit and leaves. It is often active by day, which makes it an easy target. Not surprisingly, its brightly coloured fur is much in demand for hats and other body ornaments. As a result the cuscus is increasingly rare, and has vanished from most of its distribution over the last half-century.

Dingiso
(Dendrolagus mbaiso)

TREE-KANGAROOS are such unlikely animals that when Australian Aborigines first told European explorers about them, the adventurers refused to believe such a creature existed. When, in 1994, New Guinean tribesmen told me of a tree-kangaroo that lived on the ground, I was also dubious. Its name was dingiso, they said, and it inhabited alpine valleys below the tropical glaciers in West Papua, Indonesia, at a higher elevation than any other marsupial on earth. But dingiso was no myth, for I soon saw one with my own eyes. At about the size of a labrador dog, it resembled a miniature panda, being boldly marked with black and white.

Dingiso lives in the high mountains, where the only sound is often the wind in the grasses and the snuffling of the long-beaked echidna. Mist can descend in an instant, as can sleet or snow, which is when dingiso's eight-centimetre-thick fur coat proves most useful. It spends its days foraging among the hummocks of moss and low bushes for tender young shoots. It is the tamest wild animal I've ever seen, for it lives in such a remote location that it has never learned to fear man. It is also one of the most beautiful of all mammals, and is highly endangered, for it inhabits a very small area of high country where it is ever more threatened by both hunters and global climate change.

Dingiso

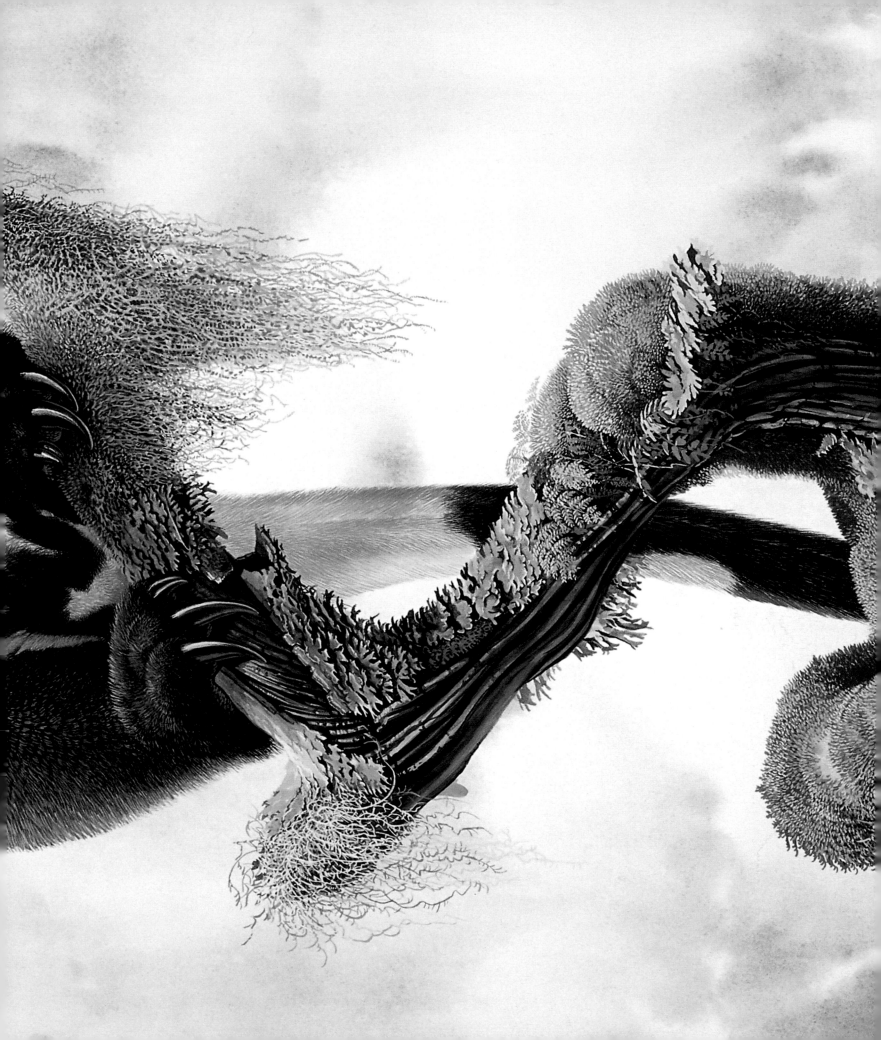

White uakari

(Cacajao calvus calvus)

THE WHITE uakari is one of the most striking of all animals. Its amazing red face with human-like ears, its coat of long, white fur that looks somewhat like a garment and its very short tail all give it a rather human appearance. It is known as 'Englishman' by the natives of the region it inhabits. Indeed it bears more than a passing resemblance to an Englishman who has been too long in the sun, or has had too much to drink. But surely the uakari's bald head has more in common with a chimpanzee's buttocks than an Englishman's face?

The uakaris are quiet, well-behaved creatures, and are the only short-tailed monkeys found in South America. The white uakari lives in a tiny, riverbound region of north-eastern Brazil, in forests known as the Várzea that become seasonally flooded. It dislikes water, the fur of its back acts as a long cape to keep off the rain. Rivers form an effective barrier to it, for the uakari cannot swim and it spurns the banks of larger rivers. It rarely leaps, perhaps for fear of falling into the waters below, but rather walks through the canopy in search of fruit, insects and Brazil nuts. It has very sturdy teeth, and you can get an idea of how powerful its jaws and teeth are by trying to crack a Brazil nut in your own mouth. Don't try too hard, though, or you will risk breaking a tooth.

White uakari

Delacour's langur

(Trachypithecus delacouri)

THE LEAF-EATING monkeys are some of the most beautiful of all primates and they are generally more peaceable and less active than other monkeys. They also often have a 'pot belly' due to their large stomachs, in which the leaves they feed upon are fermented.

   Many species of leaf monkey are both very rare and very poorly studied. Delacour's langur is a leaf eater from the forests of central Vietnam, and it may well be the most endangered monkey in all of Asia, for just 250 are thought to survive. Almost nothing has been recorded of its life history.

Golden snub-nosed monkey

(Rhinopithecus roxellanae)

IMAGINE TRAIPSING through the snows of the high Himalayas in a blizzard, gasping for breath, when suddenly an ape-like creature rises up in front of you, then walks towards the cover of a copse of rhododendron bushes. It is difficult to judge its size against the snow and stunted bushes, making the alsatian-sized creature appear much larger. No, it's not a yeti, but the animal that may have given rise to the yeti myth—the golden snub-nosed monkey.

The golden snub-nosed monkey is the largest of the temperate Asian leaf-eating monkeys, and the only one that regularly ventures up into the snow of the high Himalayas, where they forage for the leaves, buds and shoots of young bamboo. Small family groups, consisting of a dominant male and three to five females and their young, are most often encountered. As yet, no one has any idea why they have such strange, snub-noses.

In Imperial China the skin of this species could be worn only by Manchu officials, which perhaps granted the creatures some degree of protection. Its supposed efficacy as a cure for rheumatism, however, made it much sought after. Nowadays, shooting by the military and 'monkey round-ups' by entire communities of farmers have depleted the population of these strange creatures to numbers of 10,000 to 15,000.

Maroon leaf monkey

(Presbytis rubicunda)

THE ISLAND of Borneo is home to many strange primates, including the orang-utan and the proboscis monkey. One of its more attractive, though lesser-known inhabitants, is the maroon leaf monkey, which eats leaves and has a delicate stomach. Their favourite food is the young leaves of vines and some of the rarer trees, though when it cannot find these it will eat a few seeds. It cannot abide fruit, however. Eating even a banana would give it severe indigestion by altering the acid balance of its stomach, a condition that could prove fatal. To aid its digestion, and perhaps to supplement its diet with minerals, it regularly eats the clay of termite mounds, carefully breaking away the outer layers so as to consume the uncontaminated interior.

Maroon leaf monkeys live in extended family groups consisting of a dominant male, his harem of a few females, and their young. Each morning they disperse into the forest to find their favoured leaves, then regroup by afternoon for a long snooze.

Kilimanjaro guereza

(Colobus guereza caudatus)

CLIMBERS ON Mount Kilimanjaro, who traverse the forests on its upper slopes hoping to reach the shrinking snow-capped summit, are often entertained by the sight of large black-and-white monkeys sitting in the treetops. These are Kilimanjaro guerezas, which can weigh up to fifteen kilograms. Strangely, their babies are born all white, and only start to get their adult colours at three months of age.

As with the maroon leaf monkey, these leaf-eaters consumes the clay of termite mounds, but being blessed with a more robust stomach they also avidly consume fruit and flowers. Most leaf monkeys survive on the water in their food, the guerezas being no exception. There are usually around ten to fifteen Kilimanjaro guerezas in a troop, most of which are females. They rarely accept more than one male, and much time is spent grooming their long fur. Roars, snorts, snuffles, squeals and purring make up their complex communication system, while males occasionally resort to body language, flashing their genitals in an excited state as a threat to the males of other troops.

With its downturned mouth, flat nose and sagging brows, the Kilimanjaro guereza is the saddest-looking of all monkeys, and it is one of the very few to lack a thumb.

Golden langur

(Trachypithecus geei)

FEW CREATURES exceed the golden langur in the cuteness stakes. It is an inhabitant of the border region of Assam and Bhutan, and is listed as endangered, so to see it in the wild probably means to make a visit there soon.

Leaves are low in nutrients, which means that leaf-eaters must save energy. The leaf-eating golden langur is gentle and unexcitable, especially when compared with the fruit-eating monkeys such as macaques. The leaf-eating monkeys are all much of a size. This is because their poor diet limits their energy, and a smaller monkey, with its larger surface area to mass, cannot keep itself warm, while a larger one cannot reach the choicest leaves.

Douc

(Pygothrix nemaeus)

THE DOUC, an inhabitant the tropical rainforests of Laos and Vietnam, was a casualty of the Vietnam war. The American military dropped defoliants such as Agent Orange over its forest home in such quantities that it has caused a long-term decline in this creature's birth rate. Along with deaths caused by the wholesale bombing and shooting of the war years, this has severely limited the population of this most beautiful of monkeys, perhaps even dooming it to extinction.

This leaf monkey is a quiet, gentle and social primate, whose calls sound like the twittering of birds. When undisturbed, family groups of between four and fifteen, led by an adult male, roam the treetops in search of leaves and fruit. Where humans are about, however, its family life suffers. Then it gets about in smaller groups, which hunters find harder to detect. When seen, though, the gentle creatures are often killed, either for food or for target practice.

Aye-aye

Aye-aye
(Daubentonia madagascariensis)

Great-tailed triok
(Dactylopsila megalura)

SOMETIMES THE environment exerts similar evolutionary pressures on different animals, so that over time they end up looking remarkably similar. A striking case involves some of the world's rarest possums and primates. The great-tailed triok is a marsupial that inhabits the middle elevations of New Guinea's mountains, while the aye-aye is a lemur restricted to the moist forests of Madagascar. Both eat the larvae of wood-boring insects, which they must detect then extract. To this end, both have very good ears in order to hear the grubs chewing deep in the tree, and both have very sharp, chisel-like front teeth to tear through the timber.

Even more amazing is the similarity of their fingers. The German name for the aye-aye translates as 'finger-beast', drawing attention the creature's almost skeletal middle finger, which bears a sharply hooked nail. In the triok, it is the fourth finger that is specialised, having become greatly elon-

gated, slender and similarly clawed. The animals use these tools to 'fish' for the grubs in their burrows.

But why do the aye-aye and great-tailed triok both have such splendid, bushy tails? Perhaps they act as a counterbalance. And why is the triok striped like a skunk? Indeed, it even smells somewhat like a skunk. The great-tailed triok is so rare, unfortunately, that only half a dozen specimens have ever been collected. No European scientist has ever studied one in the wild, so these questions remain unresolved. Until recently the aye-aye was considered to be equally rare, though surveys have now revealed that it exists in considerable numbers. One other difference is size: at three kilograms the aye-aye is six times as heavy as the triok.

Aye-ayes looks ghostly, and because the animal is nocturnal some Madagascans superstitiously believe that if one is seen near a village it must be killed or disaster will befall them.

Pallas' tube-nosed bat
(Nyctimene cephalotes)

THE ISLAND of Sulawesi in Indonesia is home to more varieties of fruit bats than anywhere else on Earth. Pallas' tube-nosed fruit bat is one of the most unusual and difficult to spot, for when it is at rest its brown-and-yellow spotted wings envelop its body in such a way that the animal resembles a dead leaf. If disturbed it peeks out from under its wings with its large, reddish-brown eyes, revealing its striking face, then takes flight. Mothers will carry their babies aloft provided they are not too large. The young clings to one of her two breasts, which are positioned rather like those of women.

Its peculiar tubular nostrils lend it a morbid, almost ghostly appearance, but it is a gentle animal and will not attempt to bite. The nostrils are probably used to allow the bat to breathe as it immerses its muzzle into large, soft fruit.

Bulmer's fruit bat

(Aproteles bulmerae)

THIS, THE world's largest cave-dwelling bat, was thought to have gone the way of the woolly mammoth, for it was known only from 10,000-year-old bones. Then in 1977 an anthropologist working in far western Papua New Guinea attended a feast held by the Wopkaimin people. He was curious as to what they were eating, so he retrieved a skull from the cooking-pit and sent it to the University of Papua New Guinea for identification. It turned out to be a Bulmer's fruit bat.

Scientists quickly returned to the cave, known as Luplupwintem, where the hunters had obtained the bats, but found it empty. In 1992 mammalogist Lester Seri and I discovered a remnant population in Luplupwintem. We heard them calling like lorikeets in the darkness far below, and after three nights finally caught one in a net set over the kilometre-deep doline.

Bulmer's fruit bats are beautiful creatures and have a peaceful disposition. They are fruit-and-nectar eaters, and doubtless play a vital role in pollinating rainforest trees and dispersing their fruit. Human hunting has caused their decline in numbers, and the bats at Luplupwintem are a reminder of the ice age, a time when these gentle giants, with their metre-wide wingspans, roamed widely in the mountains of New Guinea. When the population was last monitored in 1994, it was slowly increasing, having reached around two hundred.

Bougainville monkey-faced bat

(Pteralopex n. sp.)

IN MOST of the world's tropical rainforests monkeys, apes and possums take the larger and harder fruit. In the remote Solomon Islands in eastern Melanesia, however, a fruit bat has evolved to do a monkey's job. The islands have no native land mammals except a few rats, which has left a wide variety of ecological niches open to the bats. The monkey-faced bats have large, hard and pointed teeth, and their chewing muscles are so powerful that their skulls have developed large bony crests, meaning they can tackle food as hard as a young coconut. Their face resembles that of a primitive primate—perhaps a lemur or South American monkey— hence their common name.

So poorly known are the monkey-faced bats that at the time I write these words (in early 2004) the very largest species, which weighs up to a kilogram, has yet to receive a scientific name. Rumour has it that it might even be named for me. The belated discovery of such a large and striking creature indicates that much work has to be done before scientists have a firm idea of the diversity of life on Earth.

Long-beaked echidna

Tokoeka

Curlew-jawed mormyrid

Long-beaked echidna
(Zaglossus bruijnii)

Tokoeka
(Apteryx australis lawryi)

Curlew-jawed mormyrid
(Campylomormyrus numemius)

A DIET of worms can do strange things to any animal, given sufficient time. The curlew-jawed mormyrid is a freshwater fish from South America. It generates its own electricity and relies on disturbances to its electric field to locate its prey, which includes worms, arthropods and aquatic insects. It has an exceptionally large brain—the largest relative to body weight of any fish, and equivalent to a mammalian brain in terms of its body size—yet it belongs to a primitive group of fish known as the osteoglossiformes. Perhaps a large brain is essential for processing electrical data.

At up to a metre long from tip of beak to tip of tail, New Guinea's long-beaked echidna is the largest of all egg-laying mammals. It too has an exceptionally large brain for such a primitive mammal. Captive long-beaked echidnas soon grow very tame, and enjoy having their tummies tickled. They become familiar with their keepers and will greet them when they enter their enclosure. In the wild, long-beaked echidnas probe for worms with their long beak, then spear them with their peculiar barbed tongue. Once the worm is impaled it is sucked into the tiny mouth like spaghetti. As a result of humans over-hunting for food, however, these large and slow-reproducing animals may soon be extinct.

New Zealand's four species of kiwi have mere stumps for wings, with a tiny claw at their ends. Their feathers have degenerated into filaments that resemble hair; and they have mammal-like whiskers, and nostrils at the end of their beaks, which they use to sniff for worms and other invertebrates. The brown kiwis of southern New Zealand are now known by their Maori name—tokoeka. They still roam freely across Fiordland and Stewart Island, and are often seen by day, probing the island's forests and beaches for worms, beetles and crabs. They will even fish in the shallows when food is short.

Kiwis lay the largest egg relative to body size of any bird—a single egg weighing up to 25 per cent of the mother's body weight. If humans faced a similar task, women would give birth to babies weighing fifteen kilograms. And the egg is very rich: 60 per cent of it is yolk; a hen's egg is, by comparison, 40 per cent yolk. The young kiwi is so large at hatching that there is no need for its parents to feed it.

Curlew-jawed mormyrid

Silky anteater

(Cyclopes didactylus)

THE SILKY anteater is the true pygmy of the anteater family, being just twenty centimetres in length, and because of its size, nocturnal habits and isolated home in the treetops of tropical rainforests, it is rarely seen and remains something of a mystery. Its golden, silky fur may seem to offer camouflage or protection, but the creature is fond of resting by day in the canopy of the silk-cotton tree, and the seedpods of the tree, which consist of a ball of soft, silvery fibres, are scarcely distinguishable from a tightly curled silky anteater.

If it is set upon, the silky anteater has two enormous claws on each hand, which it jabs much like a boxer striking out at his opponent. If all else fails it spits at whatever is harassing it. The travel writer and adventurer Redmond O'Hanlon relates that the silky anteater is fond of having its tummy tickled.

Long-tailed tree-pangolin

(Manis tetradactyla)

ALL SEVEN pangolin species are covered in extremely sharp, flat hairs that look like fingernails, or the scales of fish. They are ant and termite eaters, but just why they are so handsomely armoured, while the silky anteater has the softest of fur, remains a biological mystery. In fact the pangolins are specialised carnivores, and thus far more closely related to cats and dogs than to the anteaters and armadillos that they superficially resemble.

Ant-eating creatures do not need sharp teeth or complex bone structures to obtain their food, and in adapting to their diet pangolins have developed the simplest skull of any mammal, and have lost all of their teeth. Food is gathered using an enormously long, sticky tongue, and the insects are then crushed

by tiny pebbles that the creature has swallowed and stored in the stomach.

Pangolins roll into a ball when threatened, and woe betide the predator that attempts to unravel them, for their scales are razor sharp and can be snapped up and down. Even when wearing leather gloves a human would be unable to unroll the tight ball held in place by the pangolin's strong back muscles. Well-defended, they are slow-moving creatures who take life at a leisurely pace. The long-tailed pangolin is arboreal and found from Senegal to Uganda and Angola. Native lore tells of it taking an 'ant bath' by reputedly lying atop an ants' nest and raising its scales so the ants can crawl under. The scales then close, crushing the ants, and the pangolin walks to a pool, where the scales are raised to release the crushed insects. Thankfully for their mothers, the scales of the young pangolin do not harden until their second day of life.

Orange dove

(Ptilinopus victor)

BIRDS ARE not generally hairy, nor are doves often flame orange, but Fiji's orange dove breaks the rules on both counts. Males of this small (twenty-centimetre-long) pigeon are covered in bright orange feathers that are so loose and fine as to resemble hairs. What is more, the filaments positively glow, handsomely offsetting the luminous green skin surrounding the bird's eye and beak. Female orange doves are, in contrast, dark green in colour, which is more in keeping with the fruit pigeon group to which the species belongs.

The dense forests of Fiji's remote eastern islands (Vanua Levu and Taveuni) are home to these creatures, and there they feed on small fruits, caterpillars and insects. Perhaps only in such an isolated place, where predators are rare, could such a conspicuous bird survive. Why is the male so strange? He certainly strains to stand out, for as he calls he puffs himself up to resemble a hairy, orange tennis ball, then jerks forward to cough out a distinctive *toc* sound. This, one assumes, is attractive to female orange doves.

Pesquet's parrot
(Psittrichas fulgidus)

WHY SHOULD a parrot resemble a vulture? New Guinea's bald-headed, long-billed and sombre-faced Pesquet's parrot is as large as a white cockatoo, and by studying its lifestyle we might find an answer to this question. Ornithologists observing the birds in the tall forests of New Guinea's foothills, discovered that the bird is irresistibly drawn to some very messy food. Perhaps the most distasteful item is the droppings of the huge, flightless cassowary. Its poo is like oversize human faeces, and is full of the undigested seeds of fruit. This is what the Pesquet's parrot is after, and as it digs seeds out of the waste with its long, pincer-like beak, its face is unavoidably smeared with a sticky, stinking mess. If it had feathers on its face it could never keep them clean—better to be bald if you prefer such foul food. Its baldness also helps keep it clean as it tears into soft, fleshy rainforest fruits that form the rest of its diet.

To see a Pesquet's parrot in the wild means to never forget it, for as they open their wings to take flight they transform themselves from dull, vulture-like birds into glittering gems, as their astonishing red belly and underwings contrast vividly with their black wings, back and sides.

Pesquet's parrot

Falanouc

(Eupleres goudotti)

FOR DECADES the falanouc was classified as an insectivore, but is now recognised as one of the most unusual of all carnivores. Its long, pointed face and bushy tail could easily mislead a casual observer into thinking it was a strange kind of fox, when its closest relatives are a type of Madagascan mongoose.

The fox-sized falanouc is solitary or lives in small family groups in the rainforests of Madagascar. It hunts at night for earthworms, as well as enjoying the odd insect and frog. Surprisingly, they will not touch larger prey such as reptiles, rodents or birds, nor will they eat fruit. In autumn they accumulate up to a kilogram of fat in their tails, which helps them survive through the lean winter months.

Platypus

(Ornithorhynchus anatinus)

THE PLATYPUS can be found throughout eastern Australia, from Tasmania to northern Queensland. They usually spend their days in burrows and emerge only at dusk and dawn to feed, but have been spotted during the day by sharp-eyed and patient observers.

Sometimes the platypus is chanced upon in the most unexpected way. Some years ago a farmer in the Sydney region was digging postholes for a new fence when he dug up a female in her nest nursing her eggs. She had dug a long burrow from a nearby creek that ended in the farmer's paddock, and had retreated into it to hatch her two eggs, which are attached to each other and about the size of a marble. So unexpected is this method of reproduction in a mammal that for years after its discovery by Europeans, scientists refused to believe the stories of Aborigines that the young platypus hatched from an egg. Indeed, so odd is the general appearance of the platypus that the very first specimens sent to Europe were proclaimed as elaborate fakes—the beaks of ducks sewn onto the bodies of moles.

For four to five months after it hatches the young platypus drinks a specialised kind of sweat, or milk, which is released from numerous glands on the mother's abdomen and lapped up off her hair. The creature utters a variety of noises, including an irritated, low growling sound when annoyed; and adults can be dangerous, for the males possess sharp, venomous spines on the inside of their hind legs that look like enlarged snake's fangs, and the poison they inject can seriously injure an incautious handler.

A few years ago the platypus surprised the scientific community once again. People noticed that they forage underwater with their eyes closed, yet they have no difficulty capturing fast-moving prey such as shrimps. How do they do it? The answer lies in its leathery bill—it creates an electric field, and disturbances to this indicate the presence of food.

Megamouth

(Megachasma pelagios)

EVEN IN this age of space travel monsters never before seen are occasionally hauled from the ocean depths. In 1976 an extraordinary shark over five metres long was hauled aboard a naval research vessel working in deep waters off Hawaii. The sea floor was over four and a half kilometres away, so the ship could not use normal anchors. Instead, the captain used two parachutes as sea anchors. Imagine the surprise of the crew when entangled in one was a great grey, soft-headed fish with a silver lining to its mouth. Its huge head, a mouth that has lips, and deep-set eyes, makes it eerily mammal-like. In 1983 it was named Megachasma, meaning 'huge gape', and so unusual was it that scientists classified the creature in its own family.

As of 2002 only seventeen megamouths had ever been seen, and so little known are they that, when surfers discovered one in 1988 in shallow water in Western Australia, they mistook it for a stranded whale and tried to tow it out to sea. One was later caught alive and released with a radio transmitter attached to it. It was tracked for fifty hours, during which time it migrated vertically, ascending from the ocean depths at night to feed near the surface upon jellyfish, shrimps and other small invertebrates. It presumably uses its small teeth and huge maw to sieve its minute prey out of the water. Strangest of all, though, is the discovery that megamouths swim in a vertical position, their great mouths pointing towards the surface. Despite the fact that it now has a name and that one has been tracked for fifty hours, almost everything about this most unusual of sharks remains a mystery.

Shape-shifters

In some circumstances appearances are everything, and in the animal world the same can be said for disappearance as well, for camouflage is sometimes the only defence a creature has. This is why some owls resemble tree-stumps, some parrots look like lumps of moss, and some fish look like seaweed. Ghostpipefish may look like jewels when they are laid out on a blank page, but in their natural habitat among the weeds, corals and rocks of the ocean shallows they are all but invisible. Tiny species are especially vulnerable, so it is not surprising that the world's smallest lizard looks like a twig.

Sometimes the appearance of animals seems inexplicable. Why does the tomato frog look like an over-ripe tomato?

Weedy seadragon
(Phyllopteryx taeniolatus)

Leafy seadragon
(Phycodurus eques)

ON A storm-tossed ocean beach in southern Australia, it is possible to spot a jewel-like body lying in the sea-wrack. At up to thirty centimetres long this creature will resemble a brilliant plastic toy rather than a fish, yet it is a type of fish known as a seadragon. In its home among kelp beds, their gorgeous ornamentation and bizarre body shape combine to provide the perfect camouflage.

Seadragons are as uniquely Australian as the platypus; the two known species are only found in Australia's shallow southern waters. They are related to the seahorses, and like seahorses the males incubate the eggs. Father seadragons are not as 'motherly' as seahorses, for instead of incubating the eggs in a pouch as male seahorses do, they stick them to a special patch on their tail. They can accommodate around 250 eggs onto their brooding patch. After hatching, the young make their way to sheltered, weedy bays, where they remain and feed on tiny crustaceans and other small marine creatures.

Rough-snout ghostpipefish
(S. paegnius)

Delicate ghostpipefish
(S. leptosomus)

Long-tailed ghostpipefish
(Solenostomus armatus)

Ornate ghostpipefish
(S. paradoxus)

Robust ghostpipefish
(S. cyanopterus)

COULD ANYONE, even in their most psychedelic imaginings, have dreamt up a cast of fish such as this? The five individuals illustrated here all belong to a single genus that is related to seahorses and pipefish. These creatures spend their days floating, near motionless, upside down, against a background that renders them invisible. They keep to the open waters until it is time to breed, and then they settle down on coral reefs, muddy bottoms or some other surface, changing their colour and shape to maximise their invisibility.

None of these pipefish exceeds fifteen centimetres in length, and many consort in pairs or small groups during the breeding season. They feed on tiny crustaceans, which are sucked up with their straw-shaped snout.

Oriental bay owl

(Phodilus badius)

THE TWO species of bay owl are very strange members of the barn owl family. When resting they perch lengthwise, and bear such a close resemblance to a broken, lichen-covered branch that they are all but impossible to see. After dark they take flight on their short wings, soaring nimbly through dense undergrowth in pursuit of prey. Their call is usually a soft hoot, though they can become vociferous in the breeding season.

Very little is known about these expert hiders. Their propensity to roost near water has suggested to some that they may include fish in their diet. The species illustrated here occurs across a wide band of southern Asia, from Pakistan to Java. A second species, known only from the Congo, remained hidden from the world until one bird was found in 1951.

Kakapo

(Strigops habroptilus)

ACTIVE ONLY by night, flightless and weighing a whopping 3.6 kilograms, the kakapo is a very strange parrot. Found only in New Zealand, it is very inquisitive and, according to explorers and gold-miners who kept them as pets in the nineteenth century, its temperament is akin to a dog, for it would loll around camp waiting to be fed, and was even willing to accept a pat on the head.

The male kakapo excavates shallow bowls at the ends of ridge-tops, which it uses to amplify its booming call. The bird inflates its body as it booms and the resulting call is audible for kilometres. The male can be very combative, and when there were more of them, males would often battle to the death. In nature they can survive up to a century, and they breed just once every four years.

As introduced rats, stoats and cats spread across New Zealand, the kakapo became ever rarer, until by the late twentieth century only a couple of dozen individuals survived, with the majority male and over fifty years of age. Only two females under thirty were known, and the future looked bleak. A carefully managed recovery program, which took a huge effort and millions of dollars, resulted in older females successfully raising chicks, and today over 100 kakapo live scattered on islands across the archipelago. The kakapo has been saved, but it will be a long time before its call is once more heard across New Zealand.

Tomato frog

(Dyscophus antongili)

MADAGASCAR IS the strangest island on Earth, its extraordinary lemurs and baobab trees perhaps its best known indigenous life. Yet few know of its spectacular frogs. Madagascar has species that mimic the spectacular poison arrow frogs of central America, Australia's burrowing frogs and Europe's toads and tree frogs, though not one of these mimics is related to the species they resemble (a striking case of convergent evolution). There is one Madagascan frog, however, that is quite unlike anything found anywhere else for, in its size and colour, it resembles a ripe tomato.

To see a tomato frog in nature, it is best to haunt, by night and in the rainy season, waterlogged ditches near the eastern town of Maroantsetra. Here they are abundant, the largest being around ten centimetres in diameter.

Kitti's hognosed bat

(Craseonycteris thongylongyai)

THIS BAT is the smallest in the world—around the size of a large bumblebee (as shown)—as well as being the world's smallest mammal. It has no tail and, as its common name suggests, its muzzle resembles the snout of a pig. Found only near the town of Sai Yoke in western Thailand, its home was once forested but today the region's forests have been completely stripped for farming.

Groups of ten to fifteen of these tiny bats can be seen resting high on the limestone walls of caves. They roost well separated from each other, not clumped together as many bats do. They become active at dusk and can be seen circling above clumps of bamboo, on the lookout for insects small enough to glean from the leaves.

Pygmy chameleon
(Brooksia minima)

THE ISLAND of Nosy Bé is something of a Lilliput for animals, for it is home to the world's smallest frog and chameleon. The pygmy chameleon may in fact be the smallest reptile in the world—it does not exceed thirty-four millimetres in length (as shown). It resembles a dead leaf as it sits motionless on bushes, its tiny limbs barely visible and head aligned with its body.

A minute, sand-coloured spot on its forehead helps individuals locate one another, and when a male and female are ready to mate she will carry her tiny lover around on her back for several days until they consummate their union under cover of darkness. They live in pairs, and the many couples in turn create small colonies that occupy around 100 square metres of primary rainforest. Unfortunately for the chameleons, Nosy Bé is well populated with humans as well, and the rate of forest clearance is such that fears are held for the survival of this tiny wonder.

Pygmy narrow-mouthed frog

(Stumpffia pygmaea)

SO SMALL is this, the world's tiniest amphibian, that a quartet of stumpffias could comfortably sit atop a thumbnail (as shown). It is known only from the quaintly named islands of Nosy Bé and Nosy Komba off the north-western coast of Madagascar, but there it is found in abundance in a variety of habitats. As befits such a diminutive and vulnerable creature, it does not expose tadpoles to the wide world; instead its eggs, which are hidden in a hole in the damp forest floor, hatch to reveal young frogs.

Exactly what a quartet of stumpffias would sound like croaking away on a thumbnail is difficult to determine, for their call is not recorded in the definitive reference book on Madagascan amphibians.

Bee hummingbird

(Calypte helenae)

AT UNDER two grams in weight it would take thirty male bee hummingbirds to equal the weight of a hen's egg. It is the smallest of all birds (as shown on this page), and a native of Cuba, where it can be found in a wide variety of habitats, from woodland to swamps, shrubby areas and even gardens. Wherever it lives it requires dense vegetation into which it can flee for protection.

Its absurdly small egg is laid in a nest made on a very thin twig, usually three to five metres off the ground. The dark-red chicks are born without feathers, but are fed minute insects at such a rate that within fourteen days they have grown their full costume. By day eighteen these tiny jewels are on the wing, having left the nest permanently to sup on the nectar of aloes, orchids, hibiscus and other plants that will support them throughout their adult life.

Shield-tailed agama

(Xenagama taylori)

ALSO KNOWN as the turnip-tailed agama, this lizard is a very popular vivarium pet. The Somali deserts that are its home are doubtless dangerous places for a lizard less than ten centimetres in length, and are even more perilous for hatchlings, which are just over a centimetre long and weigh only three grams. At such a size even a spider or scorpion is a formidable enemy, and perhaps this is why this burrowing lizard has become the ultimate tail-blocker, using its wonderfully spiny tail to block the entrance of their burrow at night. They forage by day for both plant and animal food, and in the breeding season the males can look quite spectacular, for then their throats can flush bright blue.

Feathered tree viper

Feathered tree viper

(Atheris hispidus)

FEATHERED SERPENTS are usually only met with in myths or legends. One kind of living snake, however, has such unusual scales that it looks as if it is covered in feathers. As its name suggests, the feathered tree viper is a member of the tree viper family with unusual keeled scales that help it climb reeds and papyrus in search of prey by providing extra grip on the slippery surfaces.

An inhabitant of east Africa, at around forty centimetres long it is a small snake and although venomous it is of little threat to humans. Other related vipers have equally strange scales and unforgettable names—such as the eyelash bush viper, so named because of the long scales on its head that resemble eyelashes.

Crested rat

(Lophiomys imhausi)

THE CRESTED rat of north Africa is a true rat which is closely related to the black rat of the world's suburbs and cities, yet it resembles a small skunk. Individuals vary, some boldly striped black and white, while others are brown and white, colours that are seen to best effect when it erects its mane as a warning. Then, whatever the colour combination, it is best to take care, for the crested rat has a mysterious defence.

It does not possess spines or sharp claws—instead its sides are armed with glands that make it smell and taste bad. Although no one knows for sure what its defensive fluid consists of, dogs have died after mouthing them, indicating that whatever it is, it is not good for you. Seven years is, as far as we can tell, their allotted span on this globe, during which time they seek out their vegetable food in forested and non-forested areas alike.

Habitat Specialists

SOME creatures have survived only by becoming specialists. Consider the diverse animals we mistakenly refer to as moles. Although they all live underground very few are, in fact, true moles—the marsupial mole is a relative of the kangaroo, while the golden mole is more closely related to elephants than to the true moles it so closely resembles.

The olm has retreated even further into the Earth. It survives only in a few caves in Europe, its nearest relatives being found in North America. And pity the poor Indus River dolphin. It has found refuge in a river that flows so fast that the creature can never sleep, *and* it has no eyes.

Marsupial mole

(Notoryctes typhlops)

Golden mole

(Eremitalpa granti)

Pink fairy armadillo

(Chlamyphorus truncatus)

Mole-shrew

(Anourosorex squamipes)

Star-nosed mole

(Condylura cristata)

Naked mole-rat

(Heterocephalus glaber)

BURROWING IS a lifestyle that seems to put its practitioners into an evolutionary straitjacket. No matter how the creature started out, once it embarks on burrowing, sooner or later it ends up looking like a mole. But there is plenty of diversity among the lifestyles of these creatures. The naked mole-rat, for example, is the closest thing the mammals have ever produced to a social insect, for only one pair breed in the entire mole-rat colony, and these two are far larger than their chaste fellows. They are treated like royalty, being fed and pampered, and in turn give their servants urine to drink, which inhibits their sexual activity.

The star-nosed mole is an inhabitant of eastern North America and it uses its nasal ornament, with its twenty-two pink, fleshy tentacles, to locate food. It is an expert swimmer that will forage under ice in rivers and ponds. The mole-shrew of south-east Asia hints at how an insectivore becomes mole-like, for it is less equipped for living underground than the other species depicted here, yet it remains unstudied in its mountain forests. The pichiciegos, or fairy armadillos, are the smallest of all armadillos. This one inhabits the arid grasslands and cactus fields of central Argentina, where it uses its armour-plated buttocks as a stopper to its burrow, much like a cork in a bottle. One of its odder features is its stiff, horny lips.

Most mole-like creatures live in burrows, but two actually swim through the ground. Australia's marsupial mole and Africa's golden moles are, in this respect, the apogee of subterranean evolution, for they live not in a burrow but in the ground itself. Curiously, the marsupial mole is related to bandicoots, while the golden moles are related to elephants.

Marsupial mole

Golden mole

Pink fairy armadillo

Mole shrew

Star-nosed mole

Naked mole rat

Yellow-headed picathartes

(Picathartes gymnocephalus)

SEEING A yellow-headed picathartes is the highlight of a lifetime for many bird-watchers. One of the world's rarest birds, it is found only in one of the most remote and inaccessible regions of west Africa. It is also a true relic, an ancient bird that survives only in the high humidity and eternal warmth of the equatorial jungles. An inhabitant of rocky areas, it makes its mud-nest in and around caves and cliffs, rarely venturing more than a few hundred metres from its roost. One reason for this fidelity to its nesting site seems to be the bird's preference for eating insects that have bred in bat guano, which is only found in the caves they nest in. This may also explain its bald head, which if feathered may become matted with bat poo.

Africans who know the bird say that no one should ever disturb a yellow-headed picathartes, otherwise it will lay its egg upon you. I once met an Australian geologist who, when working in west Africa, decided to have a picnic lunch in a grotto inhabited by the birds. He waved away the concerns of his assistants, who stayed outside while he ate, but as he rose to leave, he heard the flutter of wings and felt a terrible, gooey blob fall on his back. It was an egg of the yellow-headed picathartes; but whether it had dropped from a nest, or been an intentional act of revenge for disturbing the bird's peace, he could not say.

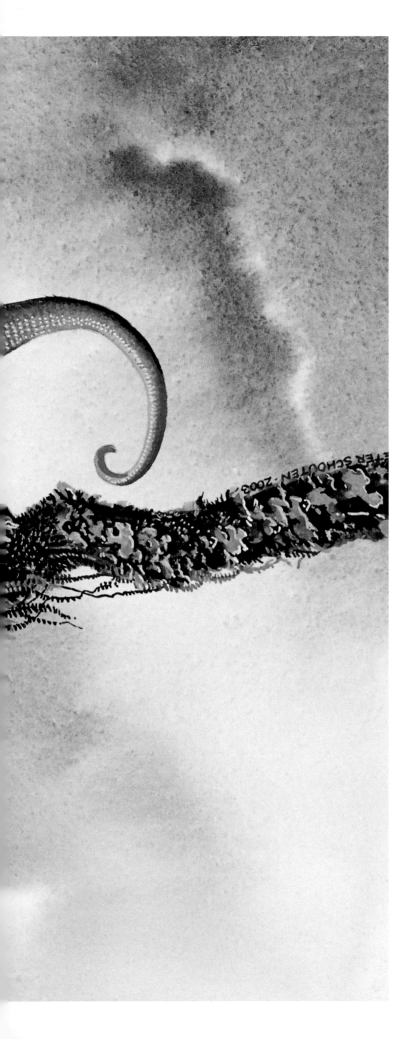

Cameroon sailfin chameleon

(Camaeleo montium)

MOST CHAMELEONS are found in Madagascar and Africa, but a few extend as far afield as India and Spain. All chameleons have peculiar grasping hands and feet, turreted and constantly swivelling eyes, and a long sticky tongue which they can shoot out at lightning speed to a length exceeding that of their body. Only a few species, however, have 'horns', and 'sails' on their back. The Cameroon sailfin is one of the oddest-looking species in a decidedly odd-looking family, and it seems likely that this is due to the fierce competition faced by males in finding a mate: the sail makes them look larger and thus more formidable, while the horns can be used in jousting contests, which take place when two males meet head-on on a twig.

The Cameroon sailfin inhabits the high, humid rainforests of Mount Cameroon, and at up to thirty centimetres long it is large for a chameleon. Like many of its kind, its colour changes with its mood; the male depicted here is in display.

Screaming Budgett's frog

(Lepidobatrachus laevis)

PARAGUAY'S CHACO region is an inhospitable tangle of scrub and cactus—a desert much of the year but which experiences a brief seasonal flooding. Anything that lives there has to be tough, and its frogs are no exception. At thirteen centimetres long the screaming Budgett's frog is large and ugly. Its loose skin, which gives it the appearance of a sock puppet, allows it to absorb extra oxygen when it is in a pond or a burrow. During the long dry season they aestivate underground.

In overall appearance it resembles the turd that a herbivorous mammal has left on the side of a muddy pool—good protection perhaps from frog-eating predators. The species gets its name from its threat display. If its turd-like disguise fails it, it rises up on its toes, inflates its body and screams loudly, mouth agape, like a woman in distress.

Budgett's frogs have some other unpleasant habits too. They bite whenever they can and are generally unclean creatures, which leaves them susceptible to infections and sores when held in captivity. They are also cannibals. The tadpoles have huge jaws and almost-square bodies, and prefer other tadpoles as food, usually beginning with the runts of their own litter. As soon as they change into frogs, their diet also switches—to other frogs.

Cape rain frog

(Breviceps gibbosus)

THE CAPE rain frog is a small, burrowing creature that inhabits sandy regions in the far south of Africa. As with Australia's water-holding frogs, when drought threatens it imbibes large quantities of water and buries itself deep in the sand under bushes, to wait for the next rains. This obscure frog is included here both because it is a splendid example of convergent evolution (with Australia's burrowing frogs), and because it is one of the silliest-looking creatures there is.

Sail-tailed lizard

Sail-tailed lizard

(Hydrosaurus amboinensis)

IF YOU had visited the island of Ambon in eastern Indonesia before the civil war put an end to all travel in the mid-1990s, you might have been offered a memento of your stay by one of the many peddlers roaming the streets. Either on foot or atop a bicycle, they carry piles of brightly coloured tropical lobsters mounted on boards, and a strange sort of lizard, painted and likewise mounted on a plaque.

This lizard, which appears quite dinosaurian, is the sail-tailed lizard of south-east Asia, a common inhabitant of the banks of rivers and streams throughout the region.

It could even be a prototype of the marine iguana of the Galapagos Islands. This animal, however, inhabits freshwater, where its spectacular tail may assist it in ascending rapids. Perhaps in a few million years they will have evolved sufficiently to be able to survive in the ocean. Then south-east Asia will have its own seagoing lizard.

Olm
(Proteus anguinus)

AROUND 135 million years ago North America and Europe were joined, and the ponds of this ancient landmass were filled with salamanders similar to the 'mudpuppies' that fishermen still occasionally hook in the southern parts of America today. Then, around 50 million years ago, Europe and North America separated. The North American mudpuppies flourished, but in Europe only one species remained. Known as the olm, it found refuge in enormous caverns in the mountains of Slovenia and so odd is it that when it was first described, in 1744 by Baron Valvasor, he thought that he had found a baby dragon. The local people knew it as the 'human fish' and seem to have regarded it with superstitious awe; the postman who delivered specimens to the Baron was described as 'brave' for handling such dubious cargo.

An olm was once placed in a small glass jar, then locked away in a refrigerator where it remained for twelve years, at a temperature of just 6 degrees Celsius. When it was removed it was still alive, and upon being dissected its digestive system was found to have completely disappeared.

They say that the olm can live a hundred years, which is perhaps to be expected of a creature that eats so rarely and lives all its life in frigid cave-water. But what does a century—36,500 days—mean to a creature that knows neither night nor day, just a long blackness varied only by the water current, which depends on the rainfall outside? It has no enemies from which to flee—and so there is little to interrupt its eternal waiting. Perhaps the olm has merely exchanged extinction for another kind of oblivion.

Indus River dolphin

(Platanista indi)

EVOLUTION CAN take creatures into realms where sleep is impossible, yet where eyes must be kept permanently closed. Such is the fate of the Indus River dolphin, an inhabitant of the Indian subcontinent. This small dolphin, which is around one and a half metres long, is very primitive, still retaining a proper neck, which has been lost in other dolphins and whales. Today it can only be found in a single 130-kilometre reach of the Indus River. The construction of dams and barriers have made it one of the rarest animals in the world, and it may well be extinct in a few decades.

The waters of the Indus run so fast that it is impossible for a dolphin to sleep without risking death by being cut to pieces among sharp rocks or trapped in a logjam. And those same waters are so murky that eyes are all but useless, so the dolphin's eyes have become covered with skin. It is not totally blind, however, for experiments have shown that it can detect the difference between night and day—a questionable achievement for an insomniac.

The Indus River dolphin swims on its side, dragging a fin-tip along the bottom, constantly moving and ceaselessly echo-locating, moving forever in a counter-clockwise direction. No one really understands why this is so, nor why the air from its blowhole smells so foully of excreta.

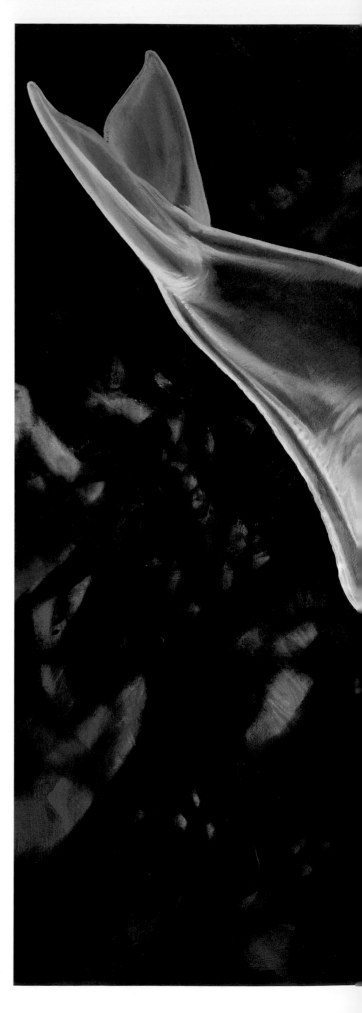

Asian giant softshell turtle

(Pelochelys cantori)

WE THINK of turtles and tortoises as creatures encased in hard shells, but there is one group, known as the family Trionychidae, that is not so protected. Their shells are instead flexible and leathery in texture. The Asian giant softshell turtle is the giant of this family, growing to a metre across—the size of an average sea turtle—and paradoxically its large size has impeded studies of it, for very few scientists have been willing to lug specimens to museums. As a result, we are still uncertain as to how many species of giant softshell turtles there are. Variability in appearance throughout their vast range in eastern and southern Asia, however, suggests that what was thought of as a single species may in fact be many.

Softshell turtles will eat almost anything—those living in the Ganges feed on the human corpses that are thrown into the river—and they thrive in grossly polluted rivers. Some even live in the putrid urban canals of cities such as Canton and Jakarta. Much about this creature remains enigmatic. Scientists speculate that it can stay submerged for extended periods by absorbing oxygen through some part of its body, and indeed a distant relative in Australia can 'breathe' through its rectum. And then there is its strange head, with its wrinkled neck and pig-like nasal appendage, which may be to allow the creature to breathe without bringing its head to the surface. Fundamental to its mystery, however, is why it has dispensed with the protection of a hard shell.

The Vertical Ocean

THE ocean is so deep that it offers nearly twice the vertical distance as that offered by the world's mountains. It is, on a kilogram-for-kilogram basis, home to most of the world's animals, and many of its inhabitants are every bit as specialised for living at a particular level below the surface as are the creatures of the mountain ranges. Many also migrate, approaching the surface every night, and returning to the depths with the dawn.

In the eternal gloom of the deep ocean lives a cast of creatures that seem scarcely believable. Their lives are lived under great constraint, for barely enough food drifts down from the sunlit layers above to keep even the most miserly eater alive. Some are forced to dissolve their skeletons in order to find the nutrients needed to lay eggs, while others may only eat once a year. Most bizarre of all are the net-devils or deep-sea angler fish. The ones depicted here are all female. If you peer closely enough, though, you might see a wart-like growth on some. This is the male, which evolution has reduced to little more than a parasitic testicle.

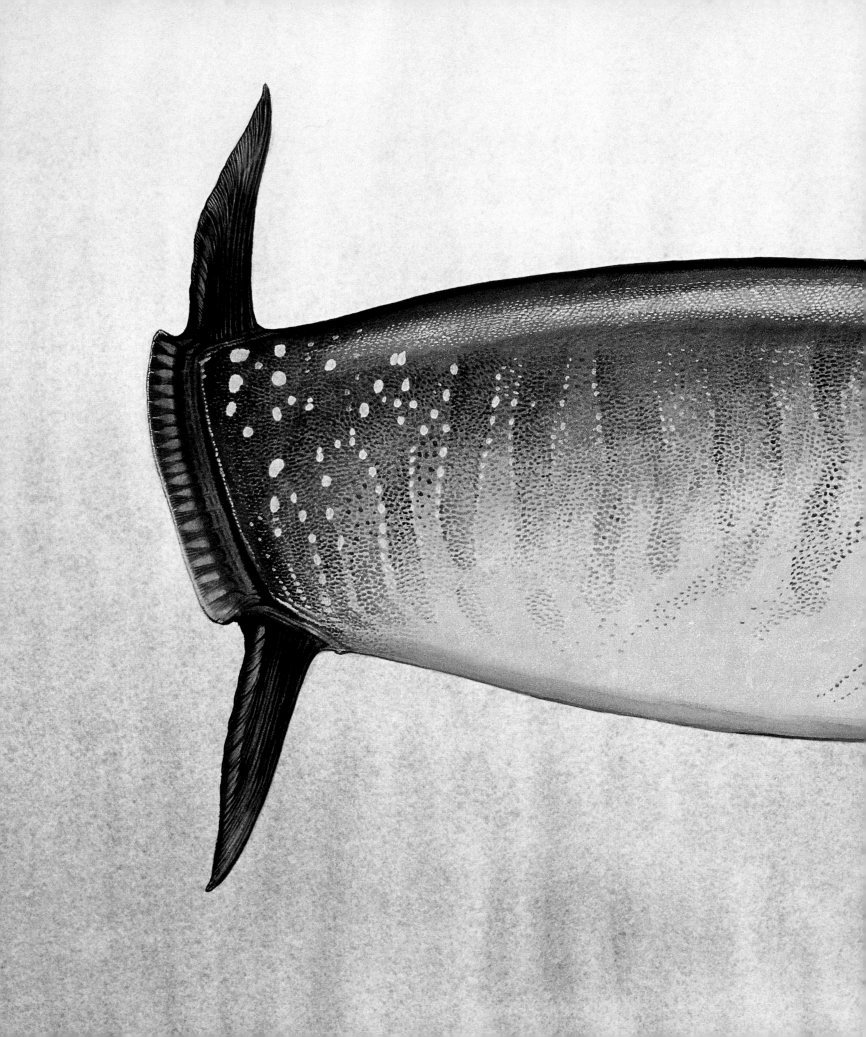

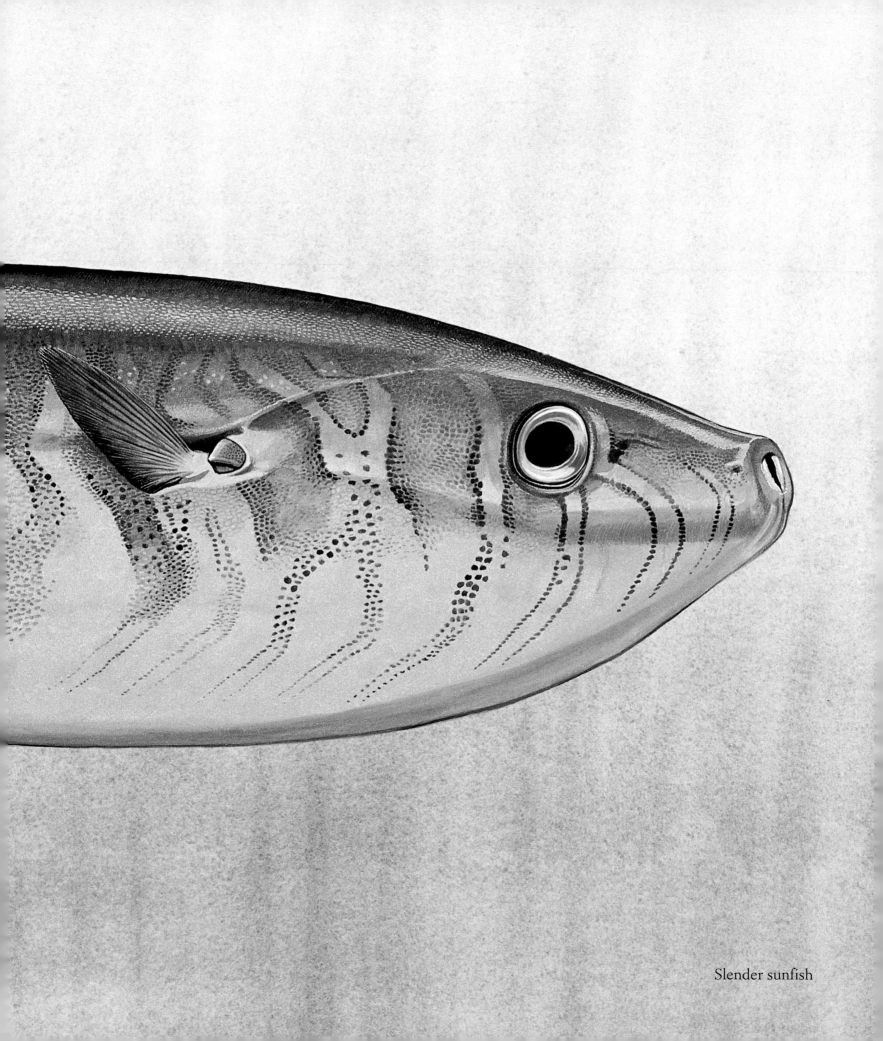

Slender sunfish

Slender sunfish

(Ranzania laevis)

THE SUNFISHES are toadfish relatives that have taken to life in the blue-water oceans. As their other popular name 'headfish' suggests, in the evolutionary process they have been reduced to little more than a floating head, having entirely lost their tail ends. Their skin has also become very tough—a veritable carapace—which perhaps helps defend them from attack by sharks.

The slender sunfish is an ancient relative of the giant sunfish or mola—one of the largest bony fish ever to have lived, though it only grows to seventy-five centimetres. A surface-dweller, the slender sunfish floats in the Atlantic and Pacific oceans, using its bizarre mouth—jaws have twisted through 90 degrees to form a vertical slit—to feed on planktonic crustaceans. It is an ancient creature, with ancestors stretching back at least 10 million years.

Wingfish
(Pteraclis velifera)

THE WINGFISH reminds me of a herring dressed up for Mardi Gras, for take away its resplendent metallic fins and it is nothing more than a silvery herring-like fish. It grows up to half a metre long, and folds away its fins into grooves that run along its back and belly. The oversized fins appear to serve no function in swimming, but may play a defensive role by make the fish appear far larger than it is. It can be found in oceans from South Africa to New Zealand.

When alive the wingfish's body is a shimmering metallic silver colour, but this rapidly rubs off after death, leaving preserved specimens a flat brown.

Strap-toothed whale
(Mesoplodon layardii)

Dense-beaked whale
(Mesoplodon densirostris)

SOME MALES give up a lot for sex—some male spiders and insects, for example, give up their lives as they are eaten by the female following copulation. Some male beaked whales, however, are victims of a fate nearly as weird, for their teeth are so affected by testosterone levels that they grow in a great arc, all but sealing their mouths shut. The function of these bizarre teeth is not clear, although the scarred bodies of adult males suggest that somehow they spar with them.

The male strap-toothed whale is the worst afflicted, having overgrown, curving tusks that, when they are fully developed, only permit the jaws to open a few centimetres. How can these enormous creatures—which reach seven metres in length—when thus handicapped, obtain enough food? It seems likely that they use powerful pulses of sound (which are also used for echo-location) to stun their prey, then suck mightily to get their food through the tiny mouth opening. If so they are not the only large sea creatures to use suction to feed; walruses have been known to remove the brains from young seals by sucking on their nostrils.

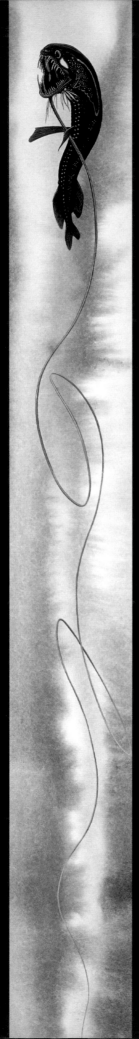

Whip dragonfish

(Grammatostomias flagellibarba)

THE DEEPER one ventures in the oceans, the stranger life becomes. Many fish that inhabit the eternally dark ocean depths have highly exaggerated body parts, but none seems as extreme as the whip dragonfish. At twenty centimetres long, it has a barbel or 'beard' that extends a metre and a half from its chin. Just what it uses this pale, brown-speckled 'whip' for is unclear. Perhaps it trawls with its barbel, hoping to attract prey. But if so, how does it reach down with its mouth to swallow it before its prey darts off?

Many deep-sea creatures possess a variety of light-emi ting organs known as photophores, and those of the whip dragonfish are peculiar. Only the male has a bright yellow light-emitting organ behind its eyes, the other light-emitting organs being a violet-purple colour in both sexes. These organs produce their light in a complex manner, for it is generated both by the action of particular bacteria that live in the luminescent organs, as well as through chemical reactions produced by the fish itself.

Crested basketfish

Crested basketfish

(Sagenapinna obriensis)

MANY FISH possess trap-like mouths, and a few have even evolved fishing poles, complete with hooks and lures. The crested basketfish appears to be unique, however, in having evolved a net with which to snare its prey. Related to tube-eyes and ribbonfish, it is a vertical swimmer in open oceans, its highly developed pectoral and pelvic fins forming an ample net. Although it has never been seen in action, it probably sieves the water with its net-like fins, or perhaps uses them to enwrap its prey. It has an ink sac in its cloaca that is used, rather like the ink sac of squid, as a defensive measure.

Stoplight loosejaw

(Malacosteus niger)

THE STOPLIGHT loosejaw looks as if it has had its throat cut. Despite its startling appearance it is widespread and relatively common, found in ocean deeps all around the world. Also known as the rat-trap fish, it is a ferocious, albeit diminutive predator, its greatest length being only twenty-four centimetres. It feeds with rapid grabs; its jaws, being stripped down to skin, bone and tendons offer little resistance to the water, thus allowing for extremely rapid action. It is a unique biter, with the strange circumstance that once it has wrapped its jaws around its prey, the victim remains outside its body! It is only when it latches on with the teeth located in its throat that it can be said to have begun to swallow its prey. From there, muscles push the food into the stomach.

The red luminescent organ under its eye indicates that it is probably a specialist predator on shrimps, which are deep red in colour. Red light is invisible to most of the creatures of the deep sea, with the exception of the loosejaws. In effect they have their own sniper scope, allowing them to see their prey while the victim remains in total darkness.

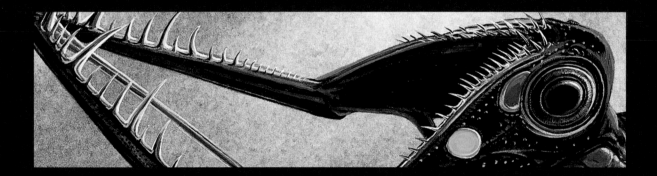

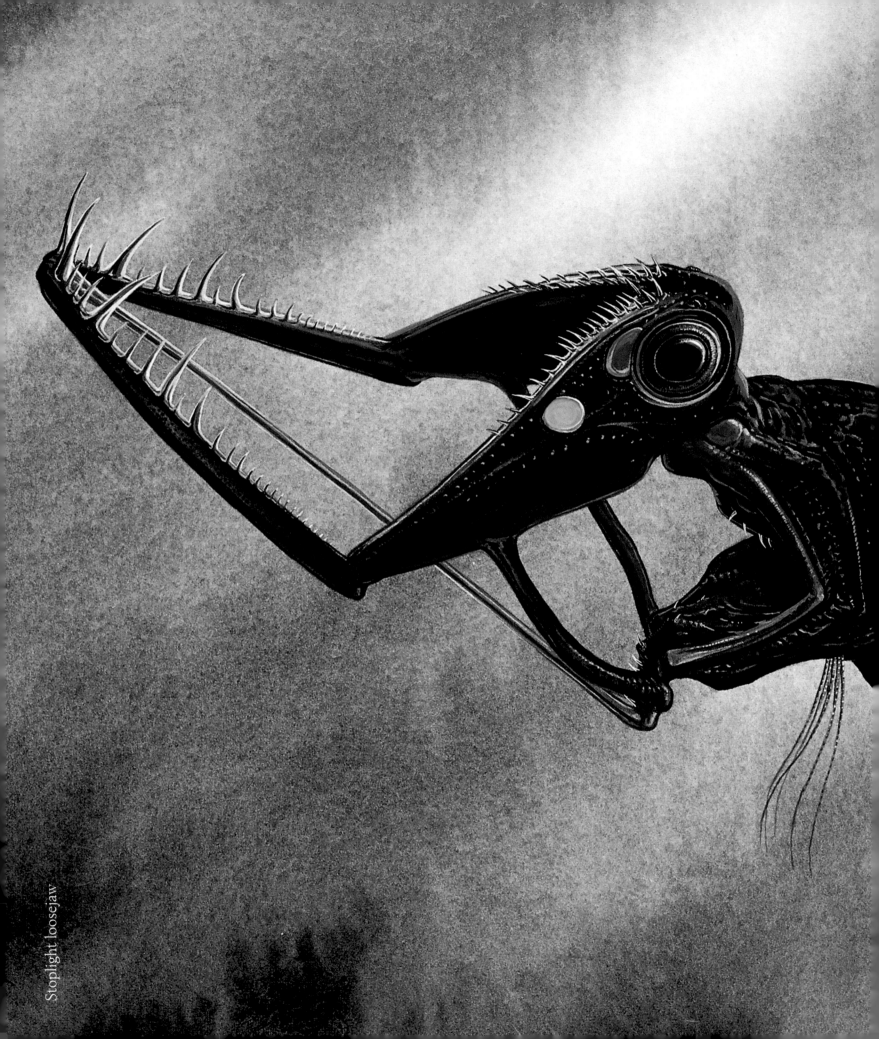

Stoplight loosejaw

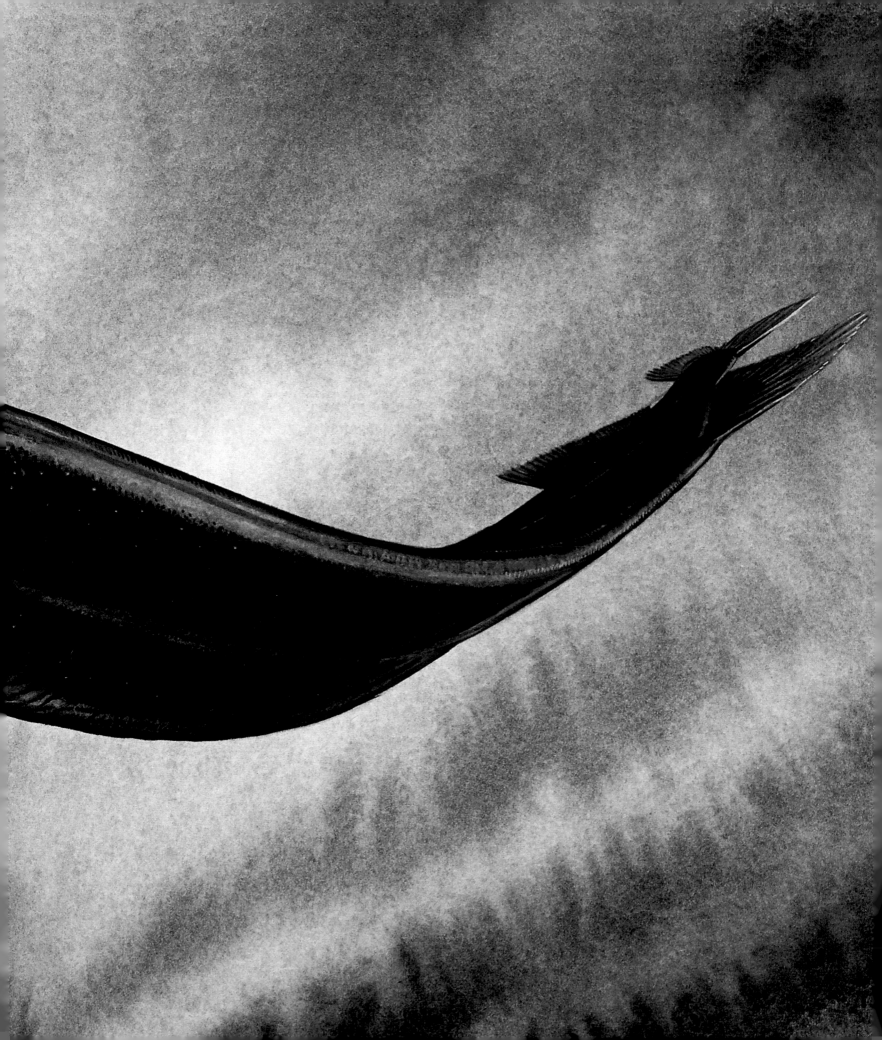

Eel tube-eye

Eel tube-eye

(Stylephorus chordatus)

LIKE THE mighty megamouth the eel tube-eye swims vertically through the ocean deep, balanced on its tail. It probably migrates 200 to 300 metres vertically upwards through the water column each night, returning to the depths by day. As it migrates, its peculiar eyes scan the slightly lighter layers of the upper ocean for food. Life for this fish must be like living with a pair of jeweller's lenses, or perhaps microscope eye-pieces, affixed to the eye—it is restricted to seeing the miniature of the sea.

It grows to nearly a metre long, though much of that is its tail. Its most remarkable feat is the ability to expand its bellows-like mouth up to thirty-eight times its resting size, a trick it employs as it feeds on copepods, which it sucks in one by one. It takes hundreds of these to provide a sufficient meal. For a human, feeding this way would be like trying to live by sucking up individual poppy-seeds.

Slender snipe-eel

(Nemichthys scolopaceus)

NEARLY TWO kilometres below the surface of the sea lurks the slender snipe-eel. It has more vertebrae in its backbone—around 750—than any other animal, and can stretch out to a metre and a half long, much of which is its thin tail. Oddly for a creature with such a long body, its anus has evolved by migrating forward and is now situtated on its throat. So slender is the fish that even the largest snipe-eel weighs less than a hen's egg. Its larvae is leaf-shaped and, strangely, shrinks slightly before transforming into the adult form. It can live for up to ten years.

It seems likely that its bizarre jaws snare the antennae of shrimps and other crustacea, for they are covered in velcro-like, backwards-pointing teeth. Many specimens held in the world's museums were spat up by larger fish caught in trawls. Fossils over 7 million years old indicate that the snipe-eel family are fish of some antiquity.

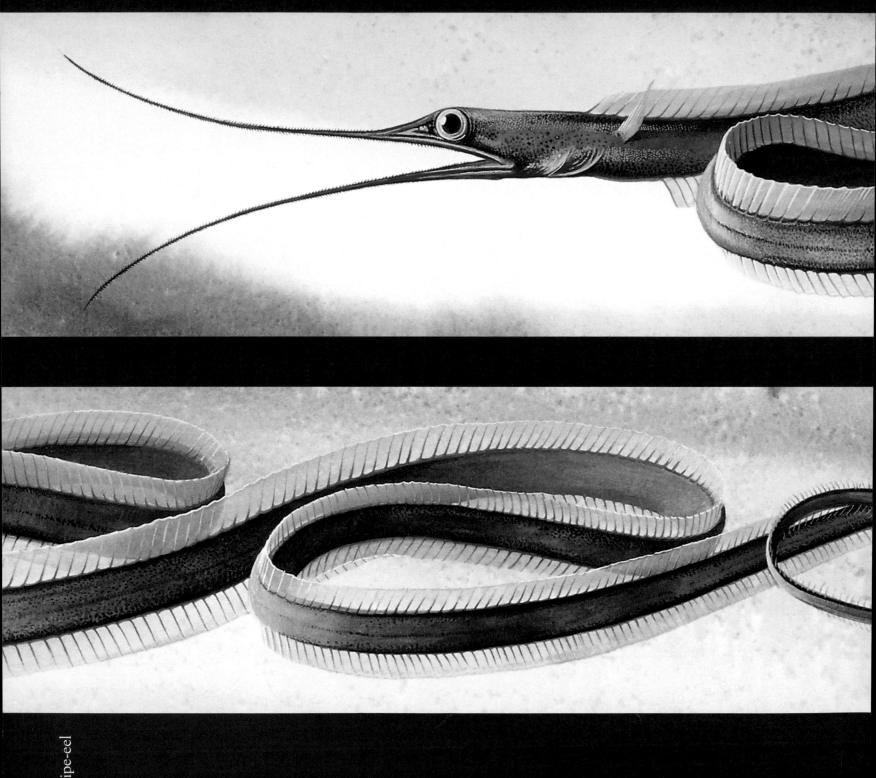

ipe-eel

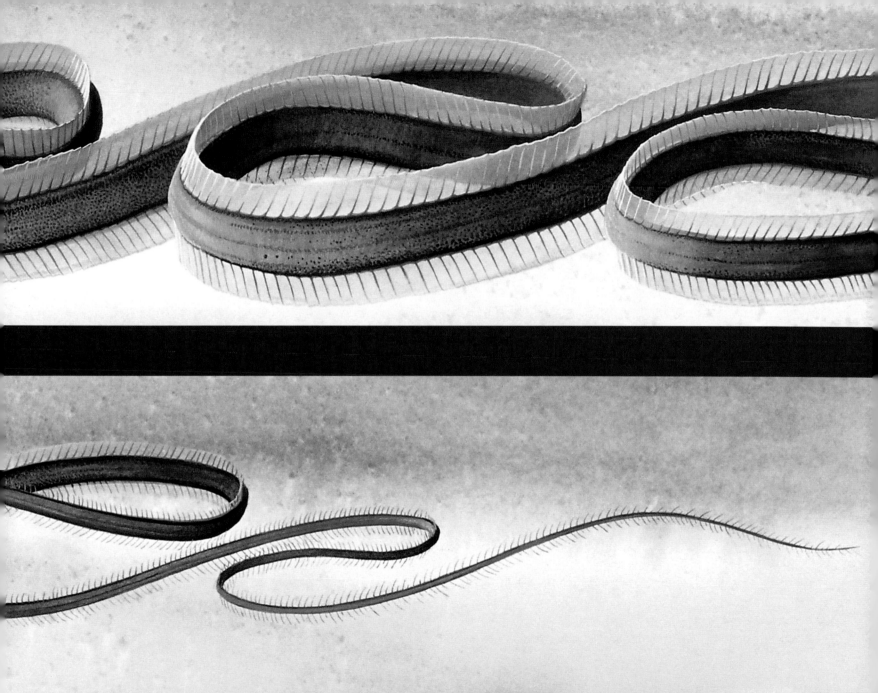

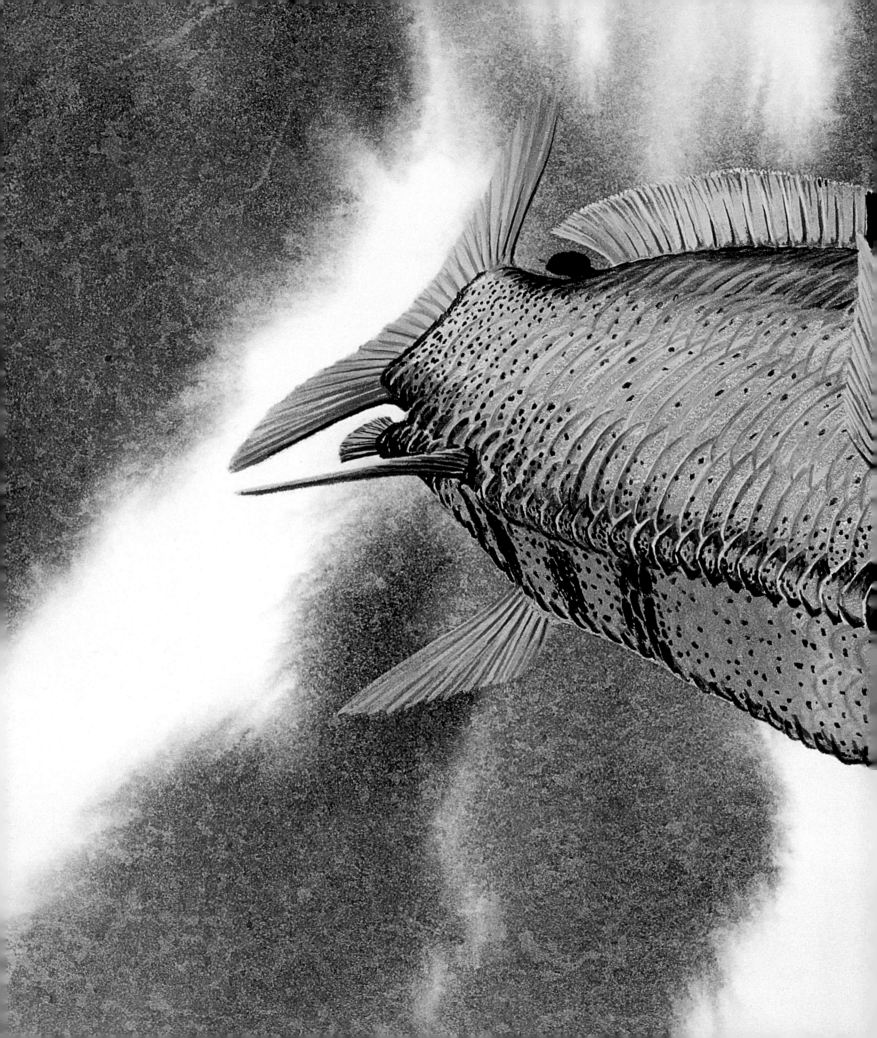

Mirrorbelly spookfish

Mirrorbelly spookfish

(Opisthoproctus grimaldi)

THE SPOOKFISHES are well named, for their eyes appear to have popped out of their sockets in fright. They are used to detect the small crustacea that make up their diet, and the retina is located deep in the head so the distance between the eye lens and retina is extreme. Even more oddly, the eyes of the mirrorbelly spookfish point straight up, while the mouth opens forwards. It is confusing imagining how they can see their prey at all.

The belly of the mirrorbelly spookfish is completely flat—like the base of a steam iron—and it glows. In the total darkness of two kilometres depth a school of mirrorbellies must be an eerie sight indeed. The luminescent organs of the spookfishes are odd. They open into the gut, and somehow special gut bacteria that emit light are transferred to the luminescent organs. These bacteria can be grown in the laboratory, where they continue to give off their ghostly glow.

Jellyfaced spookfish
(Winteria telescopa)

UP TO two and a half kilometres below the surface of the Indian Ocean lives the jellyfaced spookfish. The creature is just fifteen centimetres long and its head appears to be made of jelly. So transparent is this weird substance that you can see the veins and arteries carrying its blood to its brain and snout.

The jellyfaced spookfish looks like a short-sighted, jelly-headed herring. Why does it have a jelly-head, and how do its eyes work to catch its prey? No one knows, nor is it clear what the three tiny red dots on the snout of this mysterious fish mean.

Jellyfaced spookfish

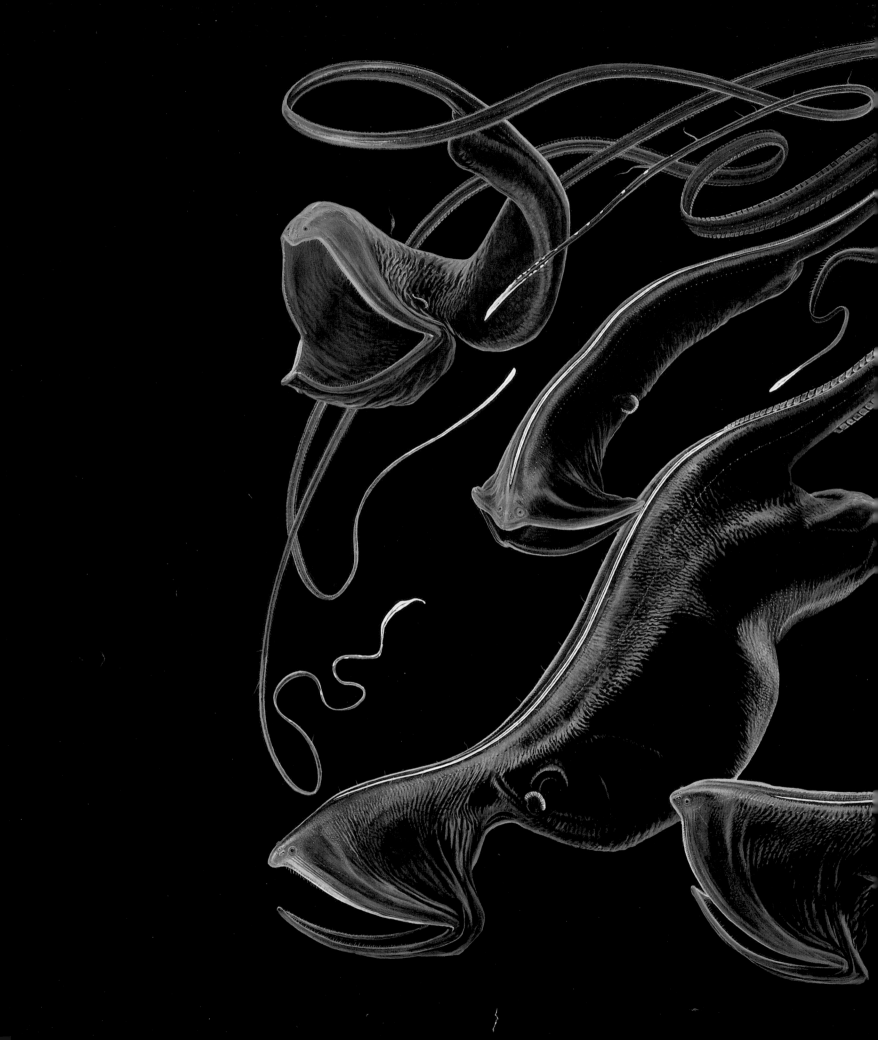

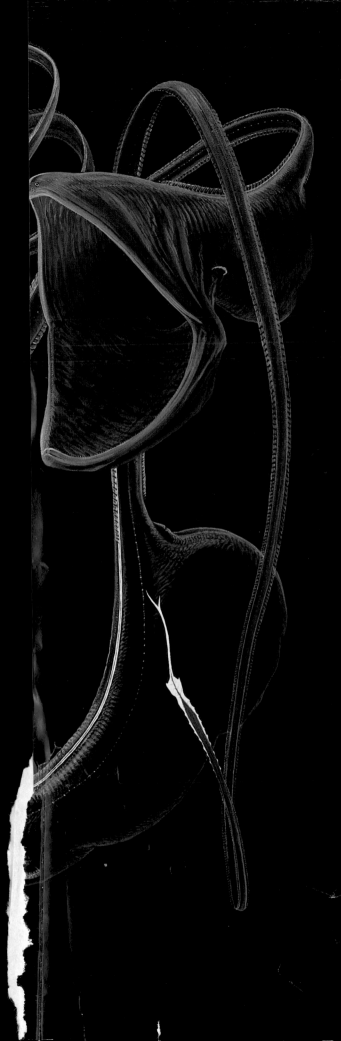

Gulpers

(Saccopharynx lavenbergi, S. schmidti, S. harrisoni,
S. ampullaceous, Eurypharynx pelecanoides)

GULPERS ARE nearly all mouth, stomach and tail, and all three organs act in concert to allow the gulpers to prey on, and swallow whole, fish as large as themselves. The fish found in their stomachs were all swallowed tail first, which is a difficult way to swallow anything spiny. We suspect that the gulpers swim so that the luminous organ at the tip of their tail floats just in front of their mouth. Then, when a fish is attracted to the organ, it is ambushed from behind by the gulper's prodigious jaws. Having fastened onto its prey, the gulper must pull itself over the fish, much like a python does when eating a deer, until finally the huge meal is safely stored away in the translucent, sack-like stomach. Their eyes are weak, so perhaps they detect the presence of their prey by changes in water pressure picked up by their hair-like filaments.

After mating gulpers undergo a metamorphosis. In order to find the calcium and energy required to produce eggs they absorb their own teeth and jaws, thus becoming little more than a sack of jelly. The umbrella-mouth gulper (*Eurypharynx*, on the top right) is only distantly related to the other gulpers. It has the biggest mouth, relative to body size, of any vertebrate.

Illuminated netdevil

(Linophryne arborifera)

THE ANGLERFISH of the deep ocean have collected a splendid set of epithets from scientists—including common blackdevil, triple-wart seadevil and illuminated netdevil. The female illuminated netdevil is rather like an ocean-going Christmas tree. Linophryne means 'toad that fishes with a net', and in this case the 'net' is brilliantly luminescent.

Indeed, this deep-sea fish has more luminescent organs than any other, and it doubtless needs them, for it lives at a depth of three and a half kilometres—a place where no light from the sun reaches at all. Despite the absence of sunlight, the illuminated netdevil's world must at times resemble a fireworks display, with explosions of light all around as predators eat predators and prey flee.

For some unknown reason the anus of young netdevil opens not along the fish's midline, as in other vertebrates, but on the left side of the belly, only later in life migrating to its proper position. The female has smooth skin, to which the male permanently attaches himself, and thereafter lives by drinking his mate's blood. Here, the small parasitic male is shown attached to the belly of the female.

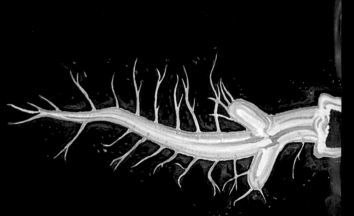

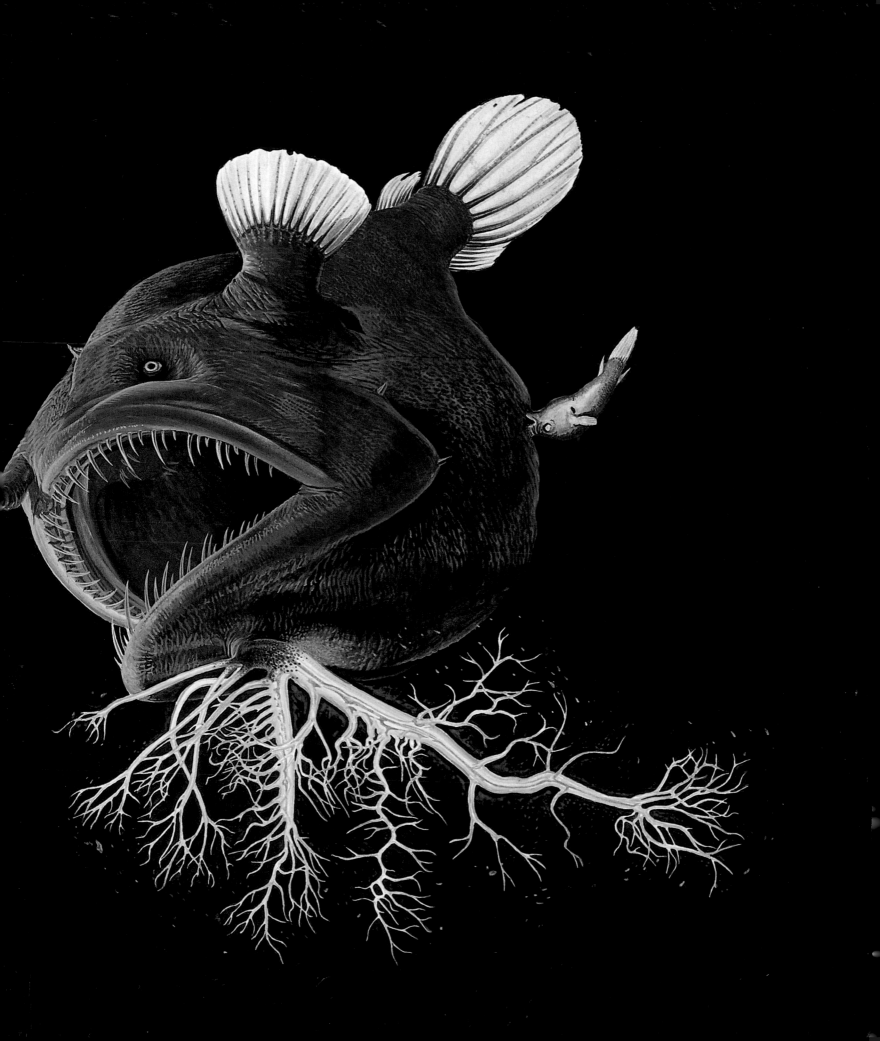

Wolftrap
seadevil

(Lasiognathus saccostomus)

ALSO KNOWN as 'Regan's strainer-mouth', the scientific name of this seadevil means 'hairy jaws', and it has one of the worst overbites in nature. The first specimen found was a female just seven centimetres long, which was brought up from the depths of the Caribbean. It is now known to be widespread in the depths of the Pacific and Atlantic oceans. The wolftrap seadevil possesses a strangely raised lateral line system. In fish the lateral line, which runs the length of the body from gills to tail fin, is used to detect changes in water pressure. In this species it may be supersensitive. It also has prominent nostrils, which suggests a fine sense of smell.

The wolftrap seadevil is a true fisherman with a long, articulated fishing pole, line and lure. The lure is illuminated and has two hooked, tooth-like structures that may function as fish-hooks. It evidently

... snares tiny prey with its lure and
... hooks and whips them into the
... cavernous mouth. It may even, like
... a fly-fisherman, cast its lure towards
... prey.

Hairy seadevil

Hairy seadevil

(Caulophryne polynema)

THE HAIRY seadevil is every bit as repulsive as its name suggests, for its vast, degenerate fins look as if they are rotting off the creature, while the tufts of 'hairs' that coat its head and parts of its body also impart a sense of decomposition. Besides giving it a general air of morbidity, these features serve a purpose, for they, along with its incredibly complex lateral line system, assist in detecting tiny changes in water pressure that indicate the presence of predator or prey.

It is a medium-sized fish for a deep-sea dweller, growing to twenty centimetres. Alone among its near relatives, the hairy seadevil has lost the luminous 'bait' that tips the fishing rod in other deep-sea angler fish. In this case, the tip of the lure is clogged with a mass of pallid hairs, whose function remains obscure.

Its elaborate tactile appendages and total absence of light-emitting organs indicate that, like Robert Louis Stevenson's pirate Blind Pew (he who delivered the 'black spot' in *Treasure Island*), the hairy seadevil lives by touch, and an almost preternatural sense of changing water pressure. Floating in its frigid, dark world it waits, sightless, for passers-by. Then, when it senses some innocent creature to be within reach, the trap-like jaws open, and in a flash the baggy stomach is set to work. Afterwards, there is only an eternity of dark, silence, and digestion.

Elsman's whipnose

(Gigantactis elsmani)

GIGANTACTIS MEANS 'giant touching device' in Latin, in reference to the extraordinary nose-mounted fishing poles possessed by these curious anglerfish. As recently as 1968 fewer than thirty adult whipnoses of all species (of which there were then ten known) had been collected, and even today these large, predatory deepwater fish are little known. A chance encounter with a Japanese submersible revealed that Elsman's whipnose swims upside down with its lantern in front of it, just above the ocean bottom, perhaps to lure worms from their burrows. It has weak eyes, which may be compensated by an acute sense of smell, the males in particular having prodigious nostrils.

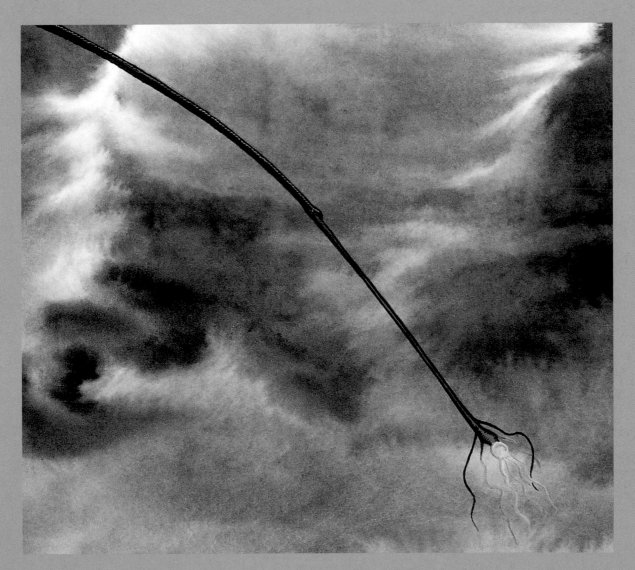

Elsman's whipnose

Pincushion seadevil

(Neoceratias spinifer)

ALL SEADEVILS have weak skeletons and flabby muscles—like the physique of a sedentary, osteoporotic old woman. And like many geriatrics it does not get a lot of exercise. Instead it waits, perhaps for months on end, suspended in its frigid, black world, for a sign that living food is near. Then, with a lightning-quick snap of its jaws, it eats.

The pincushion seadevil's teeth are jointed so as to draw prey into its venus-flytrap mouth. At eight centimetres long it is small compared with some of its relatives, and it possesses no lure or other ornaments. It does, however, have an extensive lateral line system and prominent nostrils, indicating a strong sense of smell and 'touch'. Males of this seadevil are parasites. When it encounters a female it bites her and eventually his entire head enters her body cavity. Thereafter, he receives all the requirements of life from 'mama', dispensing with gills. A male can be seen here, attached to the female near her anus.

Index